EDWARD JOHN CARNELL:
DEFENDER OF THE FAITH

John A. Sims

Library of Congress Catalog Card Number: 78-57980

Affectionately dedicated to

my three sons:

John Patrick, Mark, and Matthew

CONTENTS

CHAPTER I

EDWARD JOHN CARNELL: THE MAN AND HIS TASK

The Man

Edward John Carnell has been rightly acclaimed as one
of the great evangelical theologians of our time. From
the time of his first major contribution to philosophical
apologetics, An Introduction to Christian Apologetics
(1948), Carnell exerted widespread influence as an articulate
apologist for conservative biblical Christianity. When he
died in 1967 at the age of 47 he left behind eight books
(mostly on apologetics), a seminary which he had guided
for five of his nineteen years on its faculty, and a host of
pastors and Christian leaders whom he had taught that one
does not have to be defensive about accepting and proclaiming
the great tenets of orthodox Christianity.[1]

The contribution of Carnell to contemporary theology
consisted not only in what he so cogently wrote concerning
the faith but also in what he achieved as president and
professor at Fuller Theological Seminary. Carnell's
ambitions were seemingly twofold; to help mold a seminary
which could produce influential graduates capable of
restoring power to Protestant orthodoxy; and, through his
own writings, to put the case for orthodoxy in a respectable
intellectual position. Guided in his convictions by the
great Protestant reformers, Carnell made the authority of
Scripture the norm for orthodoxy -- defining orthodoxy

as "that branch of Christendom which limits the ground of religious authority to the Bible."[2] He saw in conservative biblical Christianity a consistent and relevant system of truth which he believed answered the basic questions facing twentieth century man.

Prior to the post World War II renaissance of conservative evangelical scholarship, the fundamentalist movement served as a rallying point for a few gifted and many not-so-gifted ideological conservatives who rushed to do battle with modernism. Many outspoken members of the fundamentalist movement exhibited such erroneous and distasteful attitudes (intoleranc separatism, anti-intellectualism, pharisaism, etc.), however, that most nonconservative theologians came to believe that fundamentalist or conservative theology did not deserve to be taken seriously.

Edward John Carnell was among those post World War II evangelical theologians who were conservative in theology but unhappy about being called "fundamentalist." Carnell wanted to restore what he believed to be classical orthodox theology, but just as importantly he desired to see a change in attitude among conservative religious thinkers.

The atmospheric change in attitude within conservative circles which Carnell labored and prayed for is nowhere better evidenced than in his inaugural address as President of Fuller Theological Seminary. In this address he called for an atmosphere of love, tolerance, forgiveness, and academic freedc in which Fuller students and professors alike could pursue

their studies. But Carnell had no intention of compromising his healthy respect for Scripture or those theological
distinctives which inhered in the seminary. He believed
that the intellectual and spiritual milieu for which he
strove should be the natural result of a seminary centered
in the Word of God.[3]

Like all men, Carnell's personal and intellectual development was heavily influenced by his life experiences. Carnell
was born to strict Baptist parents in Antigo, Wisconsin, June
28, 1919, and was reared in a Baptist parsonage. By adoles-
cence, it was evident that young Carnell was both bright
and moody. Those who knew him best during his formative
years of education remember the obvious inner conflicts which
Carnell was desperately seeking to work out. Finding his
personal sense of identity and establishing a first person
faith against the backdrop of his fundamentalist upbringing
was not easy for a bright young man like Carnell who took
everything so seriously. He saw the unfortunate inconsistencies
between those good and admirable qualities displayed by many
fundamentalists who possessed great strength of character
and conviction and those sinister attitudes and legalisms
which characterized so many during that era. Refusing to be
stereotyped or boxed into a closed system of ideological
thinking and cultic attitudes, Carnell opted for personal
freedom of thought and action.

The result was a creative and prolific pen and a reason
for the hope that lay in the hearts of literally thousands of

evangelicals whose faith stood in need of more precise
articulation. Evangelicals from every walk of life have
acknowledged their indebtedness to this seminal scholar and
educator who made them proud of their faith. The testimoni-
als of some whose lives were touched by Carnell's influence
are proof enough that his life work was both productive and
lasting. David Hubbard, President of Fuller Theological
Seminary, said of Carnell at the occasion of the unveiling
of Carnell's portrait at the Seminary in 1969:

> Edward John Carnell set a bright example for us
> in three areas: scholarship, educational out-
> look, and churchmanship. His fertile mind and
> ready pen blazed fresh theological trails as he
> sought to defend and proclaim the Christian faith
> as a world and life view. His painstaking grasp
> of the details of his field, coupled with his
> penetrating insight into the crucial questions,
> are hallmarks of the finest kind of scholarship.
> During his years as president, Fuller Seminary
> made such remarkable advances in curriculum,
> faculty appointments, library holdings and finan-
> cial stability that full accreditation was achieved.
> As much as any man, he shaped the Seminary's
> character. His love for the Church was seen both
> in his distaste for divisiveness and in his drive
> to point out and correct her foibles. A legion
> of evangelicals around the world owe to him their
> love of the faith and their loyalty to the Church.[4]

Paul Jewett, a life-long friend of Carnell's and Professor
of Systematic Theology at Fuller Seminary for many years,
spoke affectionately of Carnell when he remarked:

> While most people knew Edward John Carnell as a
> scholar and teacher, I knew him as an unfailing
> friend. I shall not soon forget our many discus-
> sions in philosophy and theology during our student
> days together in college, seminary, and graduate
> school as well as during our years of teaching
> together; but most of all I shall cherish the
> memory of his kindness, too personal to be elab-
> orated, too genuine to be left to the oblivion
> of silence.[5]

James P. Morgan, a former student of Carnell's who has
since taught Systematic Theology himself, spoke for many young
evangelicals who went to Fuller for the opportunity to sit
under Carnell:

> As an undergraduate I heard Dr. Carnell speak but
> once, and on the strength of that one encounter I
> came to Fuller Seminary. He made it possible for
> many of us to believe in a future for evangelical
> theology. In our moments of doubt and frustration
> he would speak, and faith in that future would be
> possible once again. He set the theological stand-
> ard for all of us; whether we agreed or disagreed
> with his point of view, he was the man by whom we
> measured our thinking. Again and again in the
> parish ministry, situations would evoke memory of
> a theme, an insight, an illustration, and our in-
> debtedness to Dr. Carnell became apparent. His
> shadow lies long over the lives of all of us who
> were granted the privilege of sitting in his class-
> room.[6]

Carnell never seemed to tire of talking and writing about
Christian apologetics. Based on his academic and writing
interests, he had a life-long penchant for apologetics.
Carnell first attended Wheaton College where he received a
B.A. degree in philosophy. At Wheaton, Carnell was heavily
influenced by Gordon Clark, a Christian rationalist who had
an interest in apologetical concerns. He received his Th.B.
and Th.M. degrees from Westminster Theological Seminary with
an apologetics major under Cornelius Van Til. This was followed by a doctorate in Theology from Harvard University with
a dissertation which later was published under the title of
The Theology of Reinhold Niebuhr (1950). Carnell pursued
and finished a doctorate in philosophy at Boston University
under E.S. Brightman. His dissertation at Boston was later

published under the title of The Burden of Søren Kierkegaard
(1965). In his later writings, the subjects of these two
dissertations exercised a considerable influence. Carnell
first came to theological prominence while still a graduate
at Harvard with An Introduction to Christian Apologetics --
a prize-winning volume[7] which found its way into many class-
rooms as a textbook for apologetics. This publication was
followed by A Philosophy of the Christian Religion (1952).
In his chapter on Carnell, in Types of Apologetic Systems,
Bernard Ramm contrasted the two works in the following manner:

> In An Introduction to Christian Apologetics . . .
> he endeavors to show the ability of Christianity
> to be rationally satisfying. In A Philosophy of
> the Christian Religion . . . he defends Christian-
> ity on the grounds of axiology. The unbeliever
> in Apologetics is shown to be foolish. The Apolo-
> getics shows that the rational investigation of
> Christianity leaves the mind satisfied, and the
> Philosophy leaves the heart satisfied. The rational
> structure of the Apologetics reveals the inconsist-
> ency of men outside the Trinitarian Faith, and the
> Philosophy established their axiological foolishness.
> The rational argument is grounded on an application
> of the law of contradiction to the totality of our
> experience, inward and outward, while the axiolog-
> ical argument is grounded in whole perspective
> coherence, i.e., including both mind and heart,
> consistency and wisdom.[8]

Christian Commitment (1957) and The Kingdom of Love and
the Pride of Life (1960) preserved Carnell's respect for
propositional revelation and for reason as a test for truth,
but these works represented a broadening of Carnell's epistemology to include "knowledge by acquaintance" and a more
existential defense of Christianity's answer to man's moral

predicament (Christ) and his anxiety (Love). These books
contain Carnell's mature statement of Christian apologetics.

At the request of the Westminster Press publishers,
Carnell wrote one of a series of three books intended to provide contemporary students of theology with a clear statement
of three contemporary theological viewpoints by convinced
adherents. Carnell's work represented the view of the conservative theological tradition and was entitled The Case for
Orthodoxy (1960). The other two were The Case for Theology
in Liberal Perspective, by L. Harold DeWolf; and The Case for
a New Reformation Theology, by William Hordern. A collection
of previously published articles appeared posthumously,
edited by Ronald Nash under the title The Case for Biblical
Christianity (1969).

From 1945-1947 Carnell served as pastor of the Baptist
Church of Marblehead, Massachusetts, and from 1945-1948 as
professor of philosophy and religion at Gordon College and
Divinity School. In 1948 Carnell went to Fuller Theological
Seminary where he remained until his death in 1967, serving
as president for five years and, in his later years, as professor of ethics and philosophy of religion.

Before one can understand and appreciate the importance
of apologetics in general and the apologetics of Carnell
in particular it is imperative to clarify the nature of the
apologetic task and to demonstrate that apologetics is essential to the transmission of the Gospel.

An apologist's objective is to convince, and Carnell
entered into creative conversation with his contemporaries
about matters of truth and religious knowledge for that
purpose. The question of what constitutes truth and the
corollary question of the scope and certainty of religious
knowledge are questions that have been asked throughout the
history of the Church and they remain as burning issues in
our own time. To analyze and reflect on certain thinkers
who have participated in the ongoing debate, before turning
our attention more directly to Carnell, will put Carnell in
better perspective.

The Nature and Necessity of Apologetics

Christian apologetics has traditionally been viewed by
most theologians as a standard, necessary theological discipline. Sundry theologians throughout the history of the
Christian Church have followed the apostle Peter's charge
to make a defense against those who may call the Christian's
hope into account (1 Peter 3:15). The apologetic task has
not, of course, carried equal weight among all theologians;
to some the task has been central, to others peripheral, but
the burden of apologetics has been present to some degree
in all theologians who have assumed the responsibility for
transmitting intact the gospel core.

Before the necessity of apologetics can be established,
however, it is important to clarify more exactly the nature
of apologetics. Two points of clarification should be

established early: the distinction between apologetics and an apology and the fact that all forms of apologetics do not come by way of explicit apologetic statement.

The apologetic task is broader than a specific apology. It involves the overall task of setting forth the truthfulness of the Christian faith with its claim to a reliable knowledge of God. An apology, on the other hand, is corollary to apologetics; it involves a defense of the Christian faith, or some aspect of the faith considered essential, against a specific accusation or attack. The apology is the reply made in an effort to demonstrate the falsity of the charge presented. Bernard Ramm, a contemporary apologist, explains the historical derivation of the terms:

> The historical origin of apologetics is to be found in the legal procedures in ancient Athens. The plaintiff brought his accusation (Kategoria) before the court. The accused had the right of making a reply (apologia) to the accusation. The reply was an effort to show the falsity of the accusation; hence the accused attempted to "speak off" the charge. Hence we have the verb apologesthai, "to give an answer, to legally defend one's self"; and the noun apologia, "the answer given, the defense made"; and apologetikos which refers to the art or skill of making one's reply or answer.[9]

Ramm notes that many apologias appear in New Testament literature, particularly in Acts. He observes that "Paul defended himself before the mob in Jerusalem (Acts 22:1ff), before the Jewish council (Acts 23:1ff), before Felix (Acts 24:1ff), and before Festus and Agrippa (Acts 26:1ff)."[10] Apologetic activity is evident too in portions of the synoptic gospels, and in the gospel of John and the book of Hebrews an apologetic slant is obvious throughout. J.K.S. Reid

states:

> There is in fact no difficulty in identifying
> apologetic elements in the New Testament. They
> appear both early and prominently. Apologetic
> activity is built into the foundations of the
> apostolic witness.[11]

Since the apostolic era, Christian literature has been

replete with apologetics. Origen's Contra Celsum, Augustine's

De Civitate Dei, Aquinas's Summa contra Gentiles, and Butler's

Analogy of Religion are classic works. And there are others

too numerous to mention.

Apologetics is directly related to the method whereby one

commends the faith. And, since Christian truth is dependent

upon some form of knowledge, the question of the nature and

validity of the Christian's knowledge of God is basic bedrock

in Christian apologetics. Ramm describes apologetics in terms

of "strategy." He writes that, "Christian apologetics is the

strategy of setting forth the truthfulness of the Christian

faith and its right to the claim of the knowledge of God."[12]

The strategy will, of course, differ according to each apolo-

gist's interpretation of what constitutes basic Christian

truth and the manner in which one gains a knowledge of that

truth, but the problems to be dealt with remain essentially

the same (the problem of truth and knowledge).

Alan Richardson, an apologist who is particularly sensi-

tive to the contemporary dominance of rational scientific

enquiry in practically every aspect of our lives in the

twentieth century, maintains that Christian apologists must grapple with the "question of the methodology of theological science in relation to that of the sciences in general."[13] Richardson writes:

> Since we live in an age which has been taught to submit every claim to knowledge to the test of the scientific method, no approach on the part of the Christian apologists to the modern mind is likely to be effective which does not demonstrate the ability of our theological knowledge successfully to undergo that test and so to justify itself at the bar of rational scientific enquiry.[14]

Reid's view of apologetics represents yet another approach to apologetic method. He agrees with John Macquarrie who says that "Apologetics is not a branch of theology, but rather a style of theology, namely that style which defends faith against attacks."[15] There should not be, according to Reid, any absolute distinction between apologetics and dogmatics; both must speak from the vantage of a confident faith which has not loosened its hold upon essential Christianity. But, Reid admits, there is a difference in intent. Dogmatics is Sach-bezogen, oriented to the thing proclaimed; apologetics is Hörer-bezogen, to the hearer of the proclamation.[16] Reid belongs to the former orientation whereas Richardson and Ramm belong to the latter.

These different approaches are significant for theological method. Whereas Richardson sees the apologist as laboring under the burden of demonstrating to modern men that Christianity can live within the boundaries of science, literary and historical criticism, and the peculiarity of its own unique categories of thought, method, and form of knowledge, Reid responds in Barthian fashion that Christian faith must not become involved in a "game with unbelief."[17] Dogmatics, Reid insists, must not be separated from apologetics. We must construe dogmatics, the systematic statement of what faith holds, as simply another "style" of apologetics, a style grounded in the Word of God but addressed to man. Proclamation of the Word commends the faith to unbelief in the Christian and non-Christian alike. It is the gospel which provides the Divine directive for the human predicament. Reid explains apologetics in this way:

> Apologetics operates from a position of strength combined with humility: strength because it is conscious of possessing a Gospel that the whole world needs; humility because the Gospel discloses further riches as it is applied to the world and its difficulties. It consists of the positive declaration of this Gospel in the face of the facts and circumstances with which it is confronted and by which it is often opposed. Apologetics engages with confessed enemies of Christianity outside, defending it against the ignorance, misunderstanding and defamation of unbelief. It engages with the wreckers from within, defending the Gospel against heresy that would ruin or disable it. And it engages more generally in expounding the faith so that it may secure a fair hearing, knowing that it is equally important to emphasize that reason is not the whole of faith and that faith is not tenable in utter defiance of reason.[18]

Apologists speak of apologetics then in many ways: as "strategy," "methodology," or "style," but the fundamental core of problems remain -- establishing the truth of Christianity and demonstrating its right to the claim of the knowledge of God.

Most apologists would probably agree with Carnell that apologetics is an art, not a science. There is no official or normative way of doing apologetics. The Christian apologist assumes a creative role when he ventures to set forth the gospel in as relevant a manner as possible while remaining consistent and faithful to the gospel of Christ.

Many leading thinkers in the western intellectual tradition, not usually thought of as apologists, have addressed themselves to the crucial problem of knowledge and truth. And in so doing, they have traversed apologetical territory, regardless of the rubric under which their thought appeared. Ramm reminds us that

> . . . not all Christian apologetics comes with a clear label. It must be said first of all that every apologia implies an apologetics; or, every attempt to defend the faith is based upon certain tacit assumptions about the truth of the faith. Secondly, a broad philosophical treatise may virtually be an apologetics. Kant's three great Critiques represent a defense of Christianity morally interpreted. Or we may mention Bishop Berkeley who saw in his spirited defense of a spiritual universe and the destruction of materialism a vindication of Christian belief. Thirdly, apologetics may be written under the rubric of the philosophy of religion (or some similar title). Thus Brightman's apologetics is in his work, A Philosophy of Religion. B.P. Bowne preferred the older caption of Theism. F.R. Tennant employed the more ambitious title of Philosophical Theology. Mullins chose the more earthly title, Why is Christianity True? Barth's system must be unearthed from his massive Church Dogmatics. However, whatever deals with truth or with knowledge with respect to the Christian faith is apologetical in scope and content.[11]

One recent trend among Barthian theologians has been to castigate apologetics, to associate this branch of theology with arid intellectualism, natural theology, Christian evidences, or philosophical verification. But such assumptions only indicate a partial understanding of the nature of apologetics. The primary purpose of apologetics is to deal with those basic problems which affect the very foundation of the Christian faith. And there are no more profound problems than knowledge and truth. Karl Barth and other dialectical theologians have expressed their belief that an explicitly stated apologetic is not a legitimate theological activity in that they regard it as just another attempt to establish rational continuity between God and man. However, apologetics is not confined to philosophers of any school of thought. Whenever "kerygmatic" or biblical theologians opt for a gospel preached without the aid of philosophy they are dealing with apologetics no less than philosophical theologians who openly use philosophy as a handmaiden to revelation. Both are laboring under assumptions which govern their view of knowledge and truth. Properly understood, the nature of apologetics necessitates its practice by theologians who undertake the transmission of the gospel to people of their own time.

CHAPTER II

MODERN APOLOGETICAL CONCERNS

The Intellectual Climate

Theological reflection and activity do not occur in an intellectual and cultural vacuum. Contrariwise, apologetical work is stimulated and influenced by the Zeitgeist. This chapter attempts to underscore that point by noting certain influences upon apologetic method and content in modern times.

It is important for our purposes to consider the back-drop of liberal theology in order to establish certain liberal apologetical presuppositions against which devotees of American neo-orthodoxy and American fundamentalism responded during the early decades of the twentieth century. Liberal theology was certainly one of the major, if not the major, tributaries feeding the mainstream of American Protestant religious thought at the turn of this century. Neither evangelical conservatism nor American neo-orthodoxy can be adequately understood apart from some insight into the continuities and discontinuities which existed among these three major American theological movements, particularly their perspectives on the matter of religious knowledge.

15

This chapter also suggests the importance of man-centered values for apologists of our time. Edward John Carnell was an apologist who was interested in the relevancy of the Gospel but not at the expense of sacrificing its unique claims to modern culture. He believed in the unity of General and Special revelation, and he sought to ally the two in such a manner as to speak to the whole man in the totality of his fourfold environment (rational, physical, aesthetic, moral and spiritual) without compromising the truth revealed in either sphere.

The Liberal Apologetic

In defining the nature of apologetics, a contemporary Christian apologist, Alan Richardson, says that

> apologetics deals with the relationship of the Christian faith to the wider sphere of man's "secular" knowledge -- philosophy, science, history, sociology, and so on -- with a view to showing that faith is not at variance with the truth that these enquiries have uncovered. In every age it is necessary that this task be undertaken; in a period of rapid developments in scientific knowledge and of vast social change it becomes a matter of considerable urgency. Thus, apologetics as a theological discipline is a kind of intellectual stock-taking on the part of Christian thinkers, who may be described as attempting to reckon up their assets in the light of contemporary philosophical thought and scientific knowledge.[1]

So considered, much of the nineteenth and early twentieth-century liberal theology was apologetic in nature in that it was a revitalized and reformed theology designed to mediate the intellectual tensions existing between the cultural

situation and the Christian message. There has probably
never been a theological movement more dedicated to correlating Christian answers with the questions raised by
scientists and philosophers than the Ritschlian theology
which dominated Protestant thought in Germany from 1875 to
World War I and in America from the turn of the century until
as late as the 1930's.

The closing decades of the nineteenth century witnessed
the waning of Hegelian idealism. Hegel's speculative idealism was widely repudiated in favor of the critical idealism
of Kant, whose epistemology had demonstrated that knowledge
is limited to the experience of phenomena. This shift in
the intellectual climate precipitated an era of metaphysical
agnosticism and a resultant surge of historical positivism.
James Livingston observes that "the new call was not only
'back to Kant' but also back to the historical sources."[2]
It was a time of emphasis on the empirical and the historical,
and an unprecedented application of the methods of historical-
critical research to the Biblical texts and the history of
dogma resulted.

Ritschlian liberalism, with its skepticism toward metaphysics, its rejection of traditional dogma and natural
theology, and its concentration on the historical Jesus with
his ethical teachings and proclamation of the kingdom of God,
appeared to many to be the perfect expression of liberal
Protestantism. At any rate, numerous liberal theologians

were inspired by Ritschl and acknowledged their indebtedness to him.[3]

Feeling little, if any, tension between Christ and culture, many liberals believed that liberal theology had made its peace with culture. It was enticing, as H. Richard Niebuhr observed, to

> count themselves believers in the Lord but also
> . . . to maintain community with all other be-
> lievers. Yet they seem equally at home in the
> community of culture. They feel no great tension
> between church and world, the social laws and the
> Gospel, the workings of divine grace and human
> effort, the ethics of salvation and the ethics
> of social conservation or progress. On the one
> hand they interpret culture through Christ, re-
> garding those elements in it as most important
> which are most accordant with his work and person;
> on the other hand they understand Christ through
> culture, selecting from his teaching and action
> as well as from the Christian doctrine about him
> such points as seem to agree with what is best
> in civilization.[4]

The attempt to harmonize Christ and culture was not unique to Ritschlian theology. Niebuhr points out that the Christ-of-culture theme had been formulated much earlier by western thinkers anxious to exhibit Christ as the hero of their own cultures.[5] Schleiermacher, in the Speeches on Religion, was a clear-cut representative of those who found in Christ a good apologetic for the great values esteemed by democratic culture: the freedom and intrinsic worth of individuals, social co-operation, and universal peace. Like Ritschl, Schleiermacher was determined to be both a Christocentric theologian and a modern man. Karl Barth, the most noted twentieth-century critic of Liberal Theology, called this

marriage of Christ and culture "Culture Protestantism."[6]

As Niebuhr notes, the conflict seen by the "Christ-of-

culture" thinkers was not really between man and God but

between man and nature:

> Back of all these Christologies and doctrines of
> salvation is a common notion that is part of the
> generally accepted and unquestioned climate of
> opinion. It is the idea that the human situation
> is fundamentally characterized by man's conflict
> with nature. Man the moral being, the intellectual
> spirit, confronts impersonal natural forces, mostly
> outside himself but partly within him. When the
> issue in life is so conceived, it is almost in-
> evitable that Jesus Christ should be approached
> and understood as a great leader of the spiritual,
> cultural cause of man's struggle to subdue nature,
> and of his aspirations to transcend it.[7]

Substituting man's conflict with nature for man's conflict

with God, liberal theologians tended to make Christ a cultural

hero -- a model for their own ideals, institutions, and phi-

losophies -- instead of seeing him at the center of man's

conflict as victim and mediator. Post-Liberal American theo-

logians, often referred to as Christian realists, believed

liberal views concerning the nature of man and human history

were the greatest weaknesses of liberalism. Liberalism suf-

fered from a romantic evasion of the hard, tragic realities

of human life.[8]

Thus, for the most part, the liberal struggle was against

an unregenerate culture. And Christ, purportedly purged of

the docetic elements which had for centuries corrupted Christ-

ology,[9] was envisioned as the reformer of culture inasmuch

as He embodied in Himself the highest and best aspirations
of man. The liberal gospel had a clarion call to "the
cultured among the despisers of religion." Christ was, as
H. Richard Niebuhr again observed,

> . . .the great enlightener, the great teacher,
> the one who directs all men in culture to the at-
> tainment of wisdom, moral perfection, and peace.
> Sometimes he is hailed as the great utilitarian,
> sometimes as the great idealist, sometimes as
> the man of reason, sometimes as the man of sen-
> timent. But whatever the categories are by means
> of which he is understood, the things for which he
> stands are fundamentally the same -- a peaceful,
> co-operative society achieved by moral training.[10]

But then again, what theological group or tradition is im-
mune from cultural loyalty? Liberals were not unique in this
respect. Rationalists and Romantics alike had accommodated
Christ to their own time.

The strength of the liberal movement was in the fact that,
even though it may have minimized certain tenets of the faith
regarded by others as "orthodox" and necessary, it did redis-
cover and re-establish certain essential tenets, relevant
to the contemporary intellectual climate, which furnished
the church with an apologetic that sustained its prodigious
labors of proclamation and permeation. The Church owes evangel
ical liberals a great debt for their historical and social
orientation in theology, their attempt to square theology
with the claims of right reason without allowing faith to
become an excuse for intellectual laziness, and their stress
on religious experience. In an age of romanticism and Kantian
idealism the theologies of Schleiermacher and Ritschl provided the basis for a powerful and cogent apologetic.

Such Evangelical Liberals as we have just described,
Kenneth Cauthen says,

> . . . can appropriately be thought of as 'serious
> Christians' who were searching for a theology
> which could be believed by 'intelligent moderns.'
> They stood squarely within the Christian tradition
> and accepted as normative for their thinking what
> they understood to be the essence of historical
> Christianity.[11]

On the other hand, there were liberals whose connections

with traditional Christianity were much more tenuous. Cauthen

describes them as 'intelligent moderns' who, nevertheless,

wished to be thought of as 'serious Christians' in some

real sense.

> They are called 'modernistic' because they were
> basically determined in their thinking by a
> twentieth century outlook. They had no real
> sense of continuing in the line of the historic
> faith. Rather, they were conscious that they were
> introducing something new. Nevertheless, they
> believed that there were elements of permanent
> significance in the Christian tradition which ought
> to be retained. However, the standard by which
> the abiding values of the Christianity of the past
> were to be measured was derived from the presup-
> positions of modern science, philosophy, psychology
> and social thought. Nothing was to be believed
> because it was to be found in the Bible or Christian
> tradition . . . The thinking of these men was not
> Christocentric. Jesus was important -- and even
> unique -- because he illustrated truths and
> values which are universally relevant. However,
> these truths and values can be validated and
> even discovered apart from Jesus.[12]

Evangelical liberals had sought to bifurcate the findings

of the empirical world and faith into two radically different

spheres, advancements in science and philosophy being quite

irrelevant to the truth of faith. But it was inevitable

that in the modern world the methods of inductive science,

which had proved so valuable in other fields, should sooner
or later be applied to the study of theology. During the
nineteenth and twentieth centuries there were numerous
attempts to enhance theology by applying scientific methods
to its study. The summum bonum was to make theology an empirical science. As Evangelical Liberals sought to touch
base with the modern civilization by means of a relevant
Christology, empirically-minded modernists busied themselves
in constructing categories to account for the realities which
science was demonstrating to be significant. The old method
of simply deducing necessary conclusions from revealed truths
no longer held; higher criticism had revolutionized theologica
method. Theology had to prove itself worthy of empirical
methods.

Theologians like Gerald Birney Smith, Shailer Mathews,
Henry Nelson Wieman, and Douglas Clyde Macintosh set themselves to the empirical task. James Livingston explains
such an approach:

> Empirical theology begins with man's religious
> experience but, unlike the psychology of religion,
> it is not interested in the subjective states of
> personal consciousness but, rather, in that
> which is experienced, in "knowledge of God."
> Therefore, an empirical theology presupposes some
> type of realistic epistemology which can overcome
> the subjectivism which has plagued modern theology,
> since Schleiermacher and Feuerbach, without at
> the same time falling into the dogmatic objectiv-
> ism of a Barth or Brunner.[13]

Within limits, such an approach to theology is not only
valid, but necessary, claims Alan Richardson. He defends the

view that theology is an empirical science in that it has its
own categories for interpreting reality -- categories which
cannot be reduced to those of any other science or discipline.
Furthermore, Richardson points out, theology is more than an
"academic" study: it

> is the investigation at the level of empirical
> science of the facts involved in the existence
> of the believing, worshipping and witnessing
> Christian community by means of the formulation
> of categories which shall be adequate to the proper
> understanding of these facts.[14]

Christian faith, it is reasoned, must not seek to es-
cape reason if it is to be apologetically sound. It must
demonstrate its ability to bear the scrutiny of modern theological methods, carried out in the spirit of modern science.
This was part of the sympathetic contact with culture that
allowed many nineteenth and twentieth-century liberals to
maintain their status as "intelligent moderns," who also
wished to be thought of as "serious Christians." By use
of a method which strove for genuine knowledge, independent
theological categories worthy of scientific investigation,
and an openminded attitude toward its subject matter modernist
theology made its claim as an empirical science.

But in the judgment of a growing number of theologians,
"Christ of Culture" thinkers had accommodated Christian faith
to the assumptions of modern culture. With their emphasis
on the immanence of God in nature and human history, both
Ritschlian and empirical theologians believed that one
could know God by starting with man's historical or psychic

experience. Christian truth could be known <u>immediately</u> because radical discontinuity was not posited between the divine and the human.

Liberal theologians began to encounter stiff opposition during the first three decades of the new century. The turn of historical events aided militant conservatives as they called into question the validity of basic liberal tenets. J. Gresham Machen, a professor at Princeton and an ardent conservative spokesman, represented the views of many hard-line conservatives when he challenged the immanence of liberalism by calling upon liberals to return to the biblical documents upon which Christianity rested and to see there the <u>ab extra</u> revelation of God's transcendence and man's sinfulness.[15] As Edward John Carnell noted:

> Machen's case rested on the conviction that there is really only one way to determine what Christianity is, and that is by studying the documents upon which the system rests. What Christianity is can be discovered only by a meticulous study of history as given in the New Testament. There is no other source.[16]

Machen's major indictment against the modernists was their lack of historicity and their insistence on philosophical categories and presuppositions to the exclusion of biblical ones. Conservatives strongly believed that the Christian religion stands or falls on the category of revelation, and they believed that liberal theology had surrendered that essential category to philosophical and scientific naturalism. They were prepared to defend their

faith in a supernatural revelation by means of argumentation.
Many were prepared to go further, even to the rooting out
of the seminaries and pulpits those whom they considered
to be unorthodox in regard to the "fundamentals" of the faith.
It was not so much the conservative reaction, however,
as the catastrophe of World War I that marked the historical
turning point in liberal optimism. This tragic war produced
a sense of despair, particularly in Europe, which undermined
the immanence hypothesis that God was working out an inevitable progress in history. This sense of despair was
largely responsible for the birth of a dialectical theology.[17]
Disillusioned liberals such as Karl Barth, Reinhold Niebuhr,
and Edwin Lewis diagnosed the basis error of liberalism to
be its emphasis on immanence and called for a new theology
marked by transcendence, discontinuity, and a Word-centered
gospel.[18] In general, dialectical theologians[19] preserved
the liberal respect for scientific inquiry and religious
experience, and they rejected the traditional orthodox view
of an inerrant propositional revelation. But with their emphasis upon the transcendence of God, the necessity of revelation
had been established.

Renewed Emphasis Upon Revelation

The so-called fundamentalist-modernist controversy which
shook America early in this century did much to divide and
alienate conservative theological thinking from the mainstream
of theological debate. Most students of history are aware

of the battles which were waged in seminaries, religious
and secular publications, and even within the denominations
themselves. Religion was a prime topic of conversation,
and spokesmen appeared everywhere to proclaim the virtues
of their own persuasion and the vices of their opponents.

To the fundamentalist[20] it seemed abundantly clear that
"the Christian Church had been infiltrated by subversives
who would destroy Christianity from within."[21] Those of a
more liberal persuasion felt themselves to be more enlightened
They accused the fundamentalist of being irrational and narrow
minded about the "facts" of reason and experience. Fundamentalists seemed to be more interested in preserving the
doctrinal and propositional truths of Scripture which they
considered normative, while liberals seemed to think that
the only thing worth saving was the essence of Christianity,
which they felt to be more ethical than doctrinal. Liberals
called fundamentalists literalists[22] and fundamentalists
called liberals obscurantists.[23] As the smoke of battle
cleared it became evident that the division was decisive and
that no immediate solution appeared plausible.

Time, however, favored the liberals. The intellectual
community, more often than not, sided with the liberals, and
the leading seminaries eventually became centers of liberalism
By the time of the Second World War few non-conservative
theologians took fundamentalist or conservative theology
seriously.

Conservative theology stood in desperate need of a
renaissance in the post-war years when young Edward John
Carnell and a host of bright new scholars[24] rose to defend
a conservative interpretation of Christianity against the
frequent charge that it was irrational.[25] The entirety of
Carnell's first apologetic, An Introduction to Christian
Apologetics (1948), was devoted to a closely reasoned argument for conservative biblical Christianity. Carnell argued
that Christianity was more reasonable and better able to
explain the facts of existence coherently than any alternative
philosophy. As a new spokesman for conservatism, he attempted
to expose the fallacious thinking of those who said that
conservative theology was irrational.

But even though conservative and neo-orthodox theologians
alike were calling for renewed interest in revelation and
biblical studies, they were by no means in agreement as to
how either ought to be approached. The new theology[26] not
only rejected the immanence of the liberals, it also rejected
the veracity of propositional revelation as proposed by conservatives. In the view of dialectical theologians, the
conservative approach represented yet another form of continuity. Neo-orthodox theologians were often referred to as
"crisis" theologians because they spoke of revelation as
something which the believer experiences in the encounter
with God, in the moment of existential commitment. They retained the emphasis upon religious experience and scientific
inquiry which had characterized liberal theology, and in this

regard they maintained closer ties with the liberal tradition than the new conservatism.

But the common interest which both movements had in problems relating to revelation and the apologetic task of the Church pointed to what historians may someday say was the most vital theological issue in the first half of the twentieth century.

Human Values and Apologetic Method

In modern times the apologetic task has been increasingly shaped by the faith which modern men have placed in the scientific method as a means of gaining reliable knowledge. It would be folly to demean the influence of science upon apologetics in an age of science.

However, it is reasonable to propose that the greatest impact upon apologetic method in the twentieth century has stemmed from the preoccupation with man-centered values -- not from science. In this century, man has occupied center stage. Perceptive contemporary apologists have recognized the fact that far more people are interested in the concrete realities of living than in abstract ideas, speculative world views, or impersonal methods. Proclamation which lacks existential relevancy is easily dismissed as arid, authoritarian, or irrelevant. Paul Tillich and Rudolf Bultmann began their theology from the perspective of man; Tillich, attempting to correlate existential questions and theological answers;

Bultmann, by focusing attention upon man's potential for authentic being.[27] The starting point for most contemporary apologetic theology has been in the certain reality of man's humanity.

This is not to imply, however, that theologians have been telling modern men only what they wanted to hear. The prophetic writings of Reinhold Niebuhr have been apologetic in nature; yet his writings have, in many respects, been shattering. But Niebuhr has been one of this century's most effective Christian apologists because of his interest in the practical, the ethical, and the social relevancy of the gospel. Commending Niebuhr's work as an apologist, Alan Richardson observed:

> . . . Today people are more interested in living than in theories, and they will see truth in its impact upon the world of real life long before they will recognize it in the writings of the academics or even in the expositions of the preachers. To make people listen to what Christ has to say about morality, not because they have an interest in 'religion,' but because they are concerned about men at work or at leisure -- this is surely the most valuable apologetic there is in our day.[28]

J.K.S. Reid contends that it was Friedrich Schleiermacher who gave modern theology its humanistic thrust.[29] And, Reid claims, the emphasis has gone unabated. But, he fears, our deference for man may result in both an abuse of the gospel and of man's true humanity. He states:

> It is true that throughout the course of Christian thought the Gospel has been represented as being

applicable to the human situation: it is pro me
(for me), and in Christ mea res agitur (my busi-
ness is being done) . . . But so far as I know
never in the course of Christian thought has so
resolute an attempt been made not merely to fit
salvation to human need, but to discover in human
need the very contours of the salvation the Gospel
offers. It cannot be assumed that communicability
is a reliable test of truth. If it be said in
defense of the modern way of thought that a desperate situation needs desperate apologetic measures,
one may sympathize, but at the same time doubt
whether the remedy advocated contains the fullness
of the Gospel, and if not whether the remedial
measures will meet the case.[30]

Carnell was well aware of the dangers to which Reid al-

ludes -- of adventitiously confusing and assimilating the

word of men and the Word of God. But as a theologian oriented

to the hearer of the gospel he consistently chose to follow

the method of correlating gospel answers with man's theo-

retical and existential concerns. Carnell once wrote:

In our enthusiasm to build on a point of contact,
of course, we may inadvertently absorb the gospel
into elements of a world system; for we do not
know precisely where common grace leaves off and
special grace begins. But if we are to get on
with our vocation as Christians, we must accept
the risk. Truth is advanced by open dialogue,
not by silence.[31]

Throughout, Carnell's method was one of correlation;

correlating a gospel interpreted with the aid of a priori

categories with questions and concerns he believed were im-

planted in the imago Dei. Carnell never seriously questioned

the continuity between such a priori concerns as reason, moral

rectitude, and human values, which he believed were implanted

by common grace, and special revelatory answers found in

Scripture. He never considered such a method presumptuous
or dictatorial.[32] God is not divided against himself, Carnell
asserted; He does not violate by special revelation the univocal bond between time and eternity which he himself has
fixed.[33] Consequently, Carnell's apologetic method was prem-
ised upon the view that God does not negate the highest and
most noble axiological expectations in man. Radical transcendence had no place in Carnell's method. True humanism is
Christian humanism in that man's highest ideals and aspirations
find their fulfillment in the will of the God who is revealed
in Scripture.

The Development of Carnell's Theological Method

From the outset of his theological career, Edward John
Carnell was a self-conscious Christian apologist. He approached theology as one whose calling and duty it was to
defend the faith. Carnell knew, however, that there was no
official or normative approach to apologetics; the approach
an effective apologist takes is determined by the intellectual
concerns and the cultural climate of his own time. Saint
Augustine defended Christianity against accusing Romans in
one manner; Bishop Butler faced skeptics in an age of reason
in yet another. But, Carnell observed, successful apologists
share one common element; they make contact between the gospel
and culture.[34] Carnell's apologetic purpose was to make contact at those points of greatest apologetic significance without

sacrificing the uniqueness of the Christian message.

In a discussion of theological method, Paul Tillich made a distinction between two types of theology, the Kerygmatic and the apologetic, which I believe will be helpful in this discussion of Carnell's method. Tillich compared the two types thusly:

> In the Kerygmatic type the Kerygma -- the message -- is reproduced, interpreted, and organized either in predominantly biblical terms or in terms taken from the classical tradition. In the apologetic type the Kerygma is related to the prephilosophical and the philosophical interpretations of reality. An apology "makes answer" -- answers the questions asked of, and the criticisms directed against, a concrete religion. But an answer is possible only if there is a common ground between the one who asks and the one who answers. Apologetic theology presupposes the idea of a universal revelation, to which reference can be made because it is acknowledged by both sides. Here the rational element in theological method becomes most important and most intimately connected with the positive element. The way in which this connection has been and should be carried through can be called "the method of correlation."[35]

Although there was much in Tillich's method and content with which Carnell never agreed,[36] there were certain basic areas of agreement in regard to apologetic method which are useful to the present discussion. Both Tillich and Carnell worked with the assumption that it is useless to proffer an answer to a question which has not yet been asked. Apologetic theology, a corrective to premature proclamation, is an answering theology: it provides a revelatory answer to questions raised by philosophy (reason) and to more existential questions implied in the tragic ambiguities of life.

Alan Richardson agreed in principle with Tillich's

Logos doctrine that there must be a "point of connection"

in man's (believers and unbelievers) reason and conscience

to which special revelation can appeal.[37] Without

the point of connection, apologetics cannot function.[38]

Richardson claimed that the central theological tradition

of the Church supported the view that every man experiences

at least a natural knowledge of God in reason or conscience.

Consequently, apologetics has had and still has an import-

ant theological role to play:

> Whenever reason and conscience are found to be
> at work, the task of Christian apologetics be-
> comes important. This view of the validity and
> urgency of apologetics is grounded upon the whole
> understanding of the relation between revelation
> and reason which underlies and . . . is in harmony
> with the thought and the practice of the great
> theologians of the Church from St. Paul's or St.
> John's day to our own.[39]

The question of "common ground" or "point of connection"

is very important in an understanding of Carnell's development

as a Christian apologist. In his early work, An Introduction

to Christian Apologetics, Carnell conceded that there could

be common ground on the level of persons, but he admitted no

common ground between the Christian and non-Christian on

the level of systems. He noted:

> Practically speaking, the Christian is pagan
> enough and the pagan in Christian enough to
> allow for common levels of action between them.
> Theoretically speaking, however, the system
> of Christianity in the ideal and the system of
> paganism in the ideal have absolutely no area
> in common. Christianity qua system waits for
> every truth upon God; non-Christianity qua system
> waits for every truth upon non-God.[40]

As Christian apologists, Carnell, Tillich, and Richardson

agreed then that the apologetical method presupposes a defense based upon a criterion mutually established between the apologist and at least some unbelievers. Richardson admitted to no common ground, however, between the Christian apologist and those who are indifferent, those who despise truth and value, and those who exalt self-aggrandisement.[41] They need a disturbing confrontation with the Gospel proclamation, what Tillich referred to as the Kerygmatic message. On the other hand, the apologist has always found a mutually acknowledged criterion with seriously-minded humanists who have a high regard for values, Marxists who value social justice, and Muslims who acknowledge natural reason; with each of these there is a basis for appealing to either conscien or reason. The area of agreement may be small but the apologist has at least found a place to stand; he can begin his task. Richardson added:

> In so far as they (secular humanist and the Marxist) see truth at all, they see it through the shining of the Source of Light, which alone renders possible man's knowledge of truth. But their vision is cloudy and distorted; it is only an imperfect seeing, as one of those who see men as trees walking. The touch of Christ's hand has begun but has not finished its healing work upon their blind eyes. the task of apologetics may be described as that of preparing to bring their eyes to be touched again by the hand of Christ, so that they may see all things clearly. The gift of sight is always a miracle of divine grace; but this does not mean that Christians may sit still and take no trouble to make ready the way of the Lord.[42]

Carnell demonstrated an eagerness in his writings to make contact between Christian revelation and truths which non-Christians have discovered about nature and life.[43]

He believed that Christianity's best defense was not in

repudiating the possiblity of truth outside the Bible but

in a cogent demonstration to modern men of "how the gospel

answers questions which the natural man, in his search for

meaning, has already raised about himself and the world."[44]

Carnell chastised conservative Christians within his own

ranks for producing "the dreadful effect of separating the

gospel from culture. . . . As a result, the natural man

concludes that the gospel is irrelevant."[45]

In the preface to The Kingdom of Love and the Pride of

Life Carnell acknowledged the value of Paul Tillich's method

of correlation and noted that his own work had been an at-

tempt to correlate Christian claims with truths found in

culture. He explained:

> In my own books on apologetics I have consistently
> tried to build on some useful point of contact
> between the gospel and culture. In An Introduction
> to Christian Apologetics the appeal was to the law
> of contradiction; in A Philosophy of the Christian
> Religion it was to values; and in Christian Com-
> mitment it was to the judicial sentiment. In this
> book The Kingdom of Love and the Pride of Life I
> am appealing to the law of love.[46]

Carnell believed that fundamentalists were, in general,

unaware of the theological worth of general revelation. It

is unfortunate, he noted, that "when orthodoxy says that the

Bible is the only rule of faith and practice, the fundament-

alist promptly concludes that everything worth knowing is

in the Bible."[47] The result is intellectual stagnation;

fundamentalists withdraw into coteries of the cult rather
than engaging in dialogue with non-believers. Carnell believed this error was sustained by non-sequitur reasoning
about general revelation. He described the faulty logic:

> Nothing can be learned from general wisdom,
> says the fundamentalist, for the natural man
> is wrong in starting point, method, and con-
> clusion. When the natural man says, 'this is
> a rose,' he means 'this is a not-made-by-the-
> triune-God rose.' Everything he says is blas-
> phemy.[48]

Orthodoxy, on the other hand, insists that special revelation completes, not negates, the witness of God in nature.[49]
Carnell believed that

> If man is made in the image of God (as Scripture
> says he is), then conservatives ought to welcome
> any evidence which helps establish a vital con-
> nection between the healing power of the gospel
> and man as a creature who is plagued by anxiety
> and estrangement. A divorce between common and
> special grace is an offence to both culture and
> the gospel.[50]

Carnell criticized "cultic" attitudes and practices
within his own theological tradition which stemmed from a
depreciation of general revelation and the insights of the
natural man. To use the familiar types of H. Richard Niebuhr,
Carnell identified orthodoxy with "Christ the transformer of
Culture," not "Christ Against Culture."[51] As Carnell resolved
the personal and intellectual struggle over the question of
God's witness in nature, he loosed himself from the fetter
of ideological thinking. The result was a more creative
theology and broadened opportunities for dialogue with thinkers
outside his tradition who were seldom spoken to by conservative

inclined Christians.

Further, Carnell's attitude toward the unity and mission of the Church seems to have been metamorphised by his realization of the distinction between the biblical doctrines of sanctification and justification by faith. In an article written for Christian Century in 1959, Carnell confessed:

> I now realize, though once I did not, that the nature of the church is never measured by the doctrinal maturity of those who profess Christ. Doctrine clarifies the plan of salvation, but a sinner is justified by faith and repentance, not by assent to doctrine. Believers, in some cases, must overcome deeply embedded prejudices before they can appreciate either the scope or the relevance of Christian doctrine. But his deficiency, other things being equal, is no mark against the person. The want of doctrinal maturity, like the want of subjective holiness, is remedied by sanctification, not justification. when fundamentalism confined the body of Christ to those who received the system of revealed doctrine, it obscured the distinction between justification and sanctification.[52]

Clarification, then, on the questions of common ground, the relationship between general and special revelation, and the distinction between justification and sanctification was important in the development of Carnell's thought and in his use of the method of correlation.

As apologetic theologians, Carnell and Tillich shared then a common interest in correlating theology with man's philosophical and existential concerns, but they were not theological bedfellows. Their interpretation of the human predicament differed significantly: Tillich's concern was to correlate man's existential questions and concerns with a theology governed by ontology;[53] Carnell sought to provide

revelatory answers to questions and concerns governed by meta-

physical, axiological, epistemological, and moral considera-

tions. Carnell's correlation of the biblical message with

these concerns is best seen through his major books.[54]

In his first major work, An Introduction to Christian

Apologetics, Carnell wrote from the perspective of a meta-

physician, determined to demonstrate that biblical Christi-

anity is rationally sound. Ronald Nash, a philosopher who

has exhibited a keen interest in Carnell's work, said of this

work:

> Carnell offered a defense of biblical Christianity
> in terms of a rationalistic and idealistic world-
> view. Making his appeal primarily to the law of
> non-contradiction and secondarily to the facts of
> science and history, Carnell argued that Christi-
> anity provides the believer with a rational world-
> view that is internally self-consistent and that
> fits the facts of science and history.[55]

Carnell's work agreed in principle with Alan Richardson's

statement that "the task of Christian apologetics is ancil-

lary to that of Christian philosophy."[56] Christianity

did not emerge as a philosophy but as a faith; it did not

come to men in the first century with a worked-out metaphysic,

but it did come, as Richardson contended, "with the offer of

the possibility of constructing a philosophy."[57] It brought

"to thoughtful men a faith-principle which (though it is

also much more than this) is a master key, opening the doors

of rationality and understanding."[58]

Carnell spoke first then to the more theoretical problems relating to man's quest for understanding, but he also
commended Christianity as a superior answer to the practical
predicament of man -- his fear of death and his enduring
search for happiness. Alan Richardson's understanding of
the apologist's task could have easily been written by Carnell.

> The task of Christian apologetics in relation to
> philosophy is the elucidation of the nature of the
> biblical faith-principle by which our experience
> is to be interpreted as a whole. Whence is this
> faith-principle derived? What evidence can be
> brought forward to commend it to thoughtful people
> in the twentieth century? How is it superior to
> other faith-principles, such as those of Marxism
> or scientific humanism? Can it stand the test of
> examination in the light of modern scientific method?
> Is not Christian faith only an aspect of ideological
> conditioning? Above all, does it help us to a-
> chieve rationality in the attempt to understand
> our world and our experience in it?[59]

During Carnell's maturation as a Christian apologist
he dealt with the problems which Richardson outlined. He
consistently labored under the conviction that the Christian
religion can adequately satisfy the whole man in the complexity of his fourfold environment (physical, aesthetic,
rational, moral and spiritual).[60] His work as an apologist
can be seen as an attempt to legitimate that claim.

In An Introduction to Christian Apologetics Carnell
argued that Christianity is a coherent religion, that it can
pass the bar of reason without asking the heart to violate
the law of contradiciton. A Philosophy of the Christian
Religion represented an added dimension to Carnell's earlier

thought. In this work he moved to the realm of values, demonstrating that Christianity is a higher value commitment and
has more to offer than any alternative value modern man might
choose to live and die for. The most significant transition
in this book, however, was Carnell's shift in emphasis from
truth as systematic consistency or propositional correspondenc
to reality to truth as "being," (moral rectitude) -- truth
in the heart which allows the existing individual to relate
to God in personal fellowship.[61] Carnell explained that
there is more than one locus of truth:

> God has so tempered truth together that no locus
> may say to another, I have no need of you. Truth
> as reality makes up the environment for fellowship;
> truth as propositional correspondence to reality
> defines the criteria of true fellowship; while
> truth as goodness of character is the fellowship
> itself. These loci act tunefully if the whole man
> is to be harmoniously related both to the universe
> over against him and to the totality of his own
> person within.[62]

Carnell found it necessary to distinguish carefully
between knowledge by inference (adequate for logic) and
"knowledge by acquaintance" (personal knowledge). Each form
of knowledge has its proper and necessary place, but "knowledge
by acquaintance" is, Carnell attested, the highest form of
knowledge of God because the knowledge is centered in "fellowship" where spirit encounters spirit in direct acquaintance:

> The apex in the pyramid of knowledge is personal
> acquaintance with God. When the creature finds
> his way to fellowship with God, the image and
> likeness returns to the center and source of its
> being, there to enjoy that perfection of love
> which human relations can enjoy only by finite
> degrees.[63]

Appealing to a broader and higher form of knowledge, Carnell found it necessary to appeal to a higher principle of verification: the righteousness of Christ. Christ is the only means, he believed, whereby the existential man can solve the moral predicament and thereby verify Christianity, from experience, as a system of truth capable of satisfying every area of reality that an individual finds important.[64] An existential consideration of the moral predicament meant, for Carnell, more emphasis upon inwardness and subjectivity, but he was careful never to divorce subjective experience from the canons of reason.

In _Christian Commitment_, Carnell's most creative work as an apologist, Carnell carefully described what he called the "judicial sentiment" and "the third method of knowing." Taking a more existential and introspective approach than before, Carnell displayed the influence of Kierkegaard's inwardness as he built an apologetic based on the moral and spiritual environment -- an environment which he contended that all men share with God.[65] The burden of this book was that Christian commitment demands moral rectitude, but the ethical imperative (love) can only be met through faith in Christ's righteousness, God's vicarious provision for estranged man. From this moral perspective, one "becomes truth" as he meets the demands of his own moral and spiritual environment -- a demand which leads to personal despair but finally, for Christians, to a loving acceptance of Christ's righteousness instead of their own.

As noted earlier, Carnell conceded that virtue cannot
be equated with the possession of truth. In The Case for
Orthodox Theology Carnell outlined the tenets of Orthodox
theology, but more important for our purposes in attempting
to understand Carnell's theological development, he demonstrated a sharp cleavage between his own thought and the so-
called "cultic mentality" of many of his fundamentalist
brethren. He exhorted fundamentalists to transcend their
cultic mentality by abandoning

> . . . the quest for negative status, the ele-
> vation of minor issues to a place of major
> importance, the use of social mores as a norm
> of virtue, the toleration of one's own prejudice
> but not the prejudice of others, the confusion
> of the church with a denomination, and the
> avoidance of prophetic scrutiny by using the
> Word of God as an instrument of security but
> not self-criticism.[66]

The test of Christian discipleship is not assent to the
fundamentals of the faith, though Carnell never demeaned
their importance, but "works done in love."[67] Too many were
guilty of substituting detached intellectual dogmas and mani-
festos for a dynamic and demanding inner commitment of "being.

Acknowledging the limitations of philosophy and science
as a source of truth, the late Carnell moved into a more subjective analysis of Christology in his discussions of the
moral predicament. He found Søren Kierkegaard and Reinhold
Niebuhr to be profound diagnosticians of the human "sickness
unto death" and masterful proclaimers of the divine provision
of grace. In the end, Carnell was less sure of any prideful

pretension to complete biblical consistency but more sure

of the sovereign God he knew could be known through humble

trust. His mature attitude can perhaps be understood through

an evaluation he made of Reinhold Niebuhr's over-anxious at-

titude toward Billy Graham in which he pleaded for tolerance.

> The issue, it seems to me, is not whether Billy
> Graham is always biblically consistent in his
> preaching. Each of us unconsciously cultivates
> some heresy or other. The issue is whether
> Billy Graham is morally uneasy about his in-
> ability to be biblically consistent. As long as
> he is willing to know the right and be trans-
> formed by it, Reinhold Niebuhr can ask nothing
> more. And the reason he can ask for nothing
> more is that nothing more can be asked of Reinhold
> Niebuhr.[68]

The real man then is the moral man who comes into being

as he mediates eternity in time through passionate ethical

decision. But, it must be noted, this kind of truth (truth

as rectitude) only comes into being when God, not man, closes

the gap between what one is and what one ought to be. The

moral imperative (the ought) does not imply the ability (the

can) on man's part, as Kant presupposed; the moral question

raised in the moral environment has only one adequate answer --

the righteousness of Christ.

Carnell made significant use of the insights of Kierkegaard,

Niebuhr, Tillich, and Freud in developing a correlation between

man's moral anxiety and Christ's active righteousness (love).[69]

In a late book, The Kingdom of Love and the Pride of Life,

Carnell built a case for love as the law of life. He employed

the insights of psychotherapy to demonstrate the teaching of

Christ that love is the law of life and that the world of
happy children -- natural zest, simplicity, unconditional
faith and acceptance -- is a virtual kingdom of love. This
world of happy children can teach grown men and women much
about God's intentions for man's happiness. What psycho-
therapists now understand, that every man needs to be loved
and accepted, Christianity has taught since the first century.

Carnell believed, however, that in many cases contemporary theologians were giving too little emphasis to an objectively apprehended soteriology based on Christ's imputed
righteousness. God indeed says, I accept you -- but the
basis for acceptance is that Jesus bore the curse of the law
through his death on the cross.[71] Love, seen through the
historical reality of the cross, was the means of divine
acceptance in Carnell's theology. Love is the key to
"knowledge by acquaintance;" fellowship with God is not possible through intellectual detachment but only through the
experience of loving and being loved.

Asking questions from the perspective of inwardness,
Carnell came to a greater understanding of the ever-deepening
meaning of existentially-laden categories such as "truth"
and "knowledge." Christian commitment demands truth in the
inner man; it is infinitely more important to know and
enjoy fellowship with God than to contemplate God from an
existential distance.

The intellectual pilgrimage of Carnell was an arduous and exciting odyssey. The trek was arduous because it involved an inner and outer struggle between Carnell's self-location within a closed theological tradition and Carnell's personal openness to new truth. But it was exciting because of Carnell's willingness to be transformed by truth whenever he found it, and the new vistas provided by fresh insights created expanding opportunities for apologetics.

Carnell's attempts to relate the claims of the gospel to the whole man, in his fourfold environment (physical, aesthetic, ration, moral and spiritual), are described in the following chapters of this book. Special attention will be given to the correlation of questions raised in man's rational and moral environment (general revelation) and answers provided by special revelation (Christ and Scripture).

CHAPTER III

CARNELL THE RATIONALIST

Man's practical problem is the "soul-sorrow" that he experiences. By "soul-sorrow" Carnell meant that there are certain realities about our existence that are incompatible with the ideal nature of man. Man is both body and soul; the body has imposed upon man certain limitations which the spirit, through self-transcendence, seeks to overcome. Man must be able to relate his "insatiable desire for self-preservation to the realities of a death-doomed body and an impersonal universe,"[1] if he is to attain human happiness, of which peace of mind is the highest form.[2]

Added to this "practical" problem Carnell noted a "theoretical" problem which has come to be known philosophically as the problem of the one-within-the-many. "The many are the particulars of the time-space universe while the one is the logical or teleological connection between them."[3] The many are the data supplied empirically by the sense experience while the one is the principle of unity which makes sense of the whole course of empirical data. Carnell believed that the intellect could never be satisfied with the plurality of the many (things, objects, sensations, peoples, qualities, etc.) that man experiences without some unifying principle

to which one could relate the whole of reality. The task

of philosophy, for Carnell, is to "construct a rational ex-

planation for the whole course of reality."[4] One's world-

view should be able to answer adequately the problems that

plague man. As Carnell put it,

> because man is both body and soul, he is a creature
> which is subject to perennial frustration and fear.
> The soul, limited in its soarings only by the law
> of contradiction, dreams of those reposes of bliss
> and happiness which it should like to enjoy, only
> to be crushed to earth at the end of its venture
> because it is united to a frail body which cannot
> support these dreams and ideals which the soul
> sets before itself. In addition to this problem
> of soul and body, man struggles to relate himself,
> a personal being, to an ostensibly impersonal uni-
> verse. The more man meditates upon the incompati-
> bilities which exist between what he might be and
> what he actually is, the more sorrowful his soul
> becomes. Man wants life, but he is offered death;
> he wants peace, but strife and friction are his
> lot.[5]

This predicament, in which all men find themselves,

> can only be solved by successfully combining
> the ideal and empirical worlds in such a way
> that one can find hope for immortality, a rational
> view of the universe, and a proper knowledge of
> the truth.[6]

To be sure, there were alternatives, which Carnell

acknowledged, to which one could turn instead of seeking a

Christian solution to the human problem. One could commit

suicide in despair; he could resort to skepticism and pes-

simism, or he could simply try to ignore the problem.[7] But

Carnell was unwilling to admit the viability of any of these.

An adequate answer to the human predicament existed, and

Carnell believed that he, as any other Christian, had the
right to assert it: that "the God who had revealed Himself
in Scripture"[8] was the solution. This assertion became the
basic presupposition which Carnell used to support his contention that God had spoken to man in his humanity through
Jesus Christ and the written Word. By accepting the Bible
as a true revelation from God, Carnell believed that the
rational man could find a systematically consistent system
of truth capable of answering the questions implied in man's
existence:

> Immediately upon accepting the Bible as a true
> revelation from God the rational man finds great
> benefits accrue to his system of thought. The
> outlines of his doctrine of God are sharpened
> and filled in with a wealth of detail; the re-
> lationship of God to nature and to history is
> clearly set forth so that the rational man
> avoids such errors as pantheism and deism; the
> problem of a common mentality among all rational
> creatures (the eternal concepts) is solved as
> all men are creatures of God, the Author of the
> eternal concepts; and the precise relationship
> of God to personal salvation is treated with a
> luxuriant wealth of details.[9]

Basic assumptions are important because they determine
the method and goal of theoretical thought.[10] For Carnell
it was extremely important that one work with the right presupposition because one's direction and destination are
largely determined by the assumptions with which he is working.
Ronald Nash has indicated that for Carnell, as for others,
basic assumptions are comparable to a train running on tracks
that have no switches. If one is consistent, one must commit
oneself to the methods and conclusions of his starting hypothesis. One cannot change without altering his starting

point; the axiom determines the theorem.[11]

In his earliest apologetic, An Introduction to
Christian Apologetics, Carnell indicated several reasons
for including a chapter on "The Christian Hypothesis":
first, because all men, regardless of the nature of their
intellectual endeavor (even including science), must work
with certain assumptions; second, because the anti-metaphysical mood of modern empiricism challenges one's right
to consider the possibility of supernatural revelation as
a solution to the problem of the one-within-the-many; third,
because the Christian finds his philosophy in the Bible,
not simply because it is in the Bible, but because when
tested, it establishes coherency (Carnell's criterion of
truth) better than any available alternative. Testing for
truth (verification) is the means by which one can satisfy
the mind that one has made a wise choice. In speaking as one
who had put orthodox Christianity to the test and judged it
to pass the stringent examination of self-consistency (conformity to the law of contradiction) and the facts of life
(history, experience, etc.), Carnell was willing to defend
Christianity as a viable and trustworthy world-view by which
one could seek to order one's own life, that is, it is a
world-view satisfying to the rational man.

His devoting what may seem an undue amount of time and
space to the subject of "presuppositions" is justifiable
on two counts: first, because Carnell makes a positive attempt to defend conservative Biblical Christianity by using

the Scriptures as his starting point; second, by understanding Carnell as a "presuppositionalist" we gain a
better perspective of the "early" Carnell as an evangelical with interests similar to men like Carl Henry,
Bernard Ramm, and Gordon Clark. These contemporary thinkers
have likewise used the principles of "presuppositionalism"
as a tool in criticizing contending systems of philosophy
and theology.[12] Ronald Nash defines the term "presuppositionalism":[13]

> Presuppositionalism is both a negative and a
> positive approach to philosophical apologetics.
> It is a negative criticism of non-Christian and
> quasi-Christian systems of thought. In a sense,
> it is attempting to "demythologize" the thought
> of modern men, that is, unmask the prejudices
> that have made him reject biblical theism as
> well as point out the inadequacies of his sub-
> stitute for Christianity. But presuppositionalism
> is also a positive attempt to put forth a distinc-
> tive defense and exposition of biblical theism
> as well as an explanation of its implications for
> every area of life.[14]

It is to this positive aspect of presuppositionalism that
we now turn our attention.

The Necessity, Nature, and Verification of Basic Assumptions

Since Christianity is a system of thought with its own
worldview, the Christian has the right to work with his
presupposition. But, as earlier stated, the setting forth
of an hypothesis does not mean that the hypothesis is necessarily true. It must be verified by the standards of consistency and coherency which Carnell concluded are the best
criteria for truth:[15]

> What one appeals to as a controlling presupposition
> in his system is not what determines the validity
> of the act; rather, granted the starting point,
> does it produce a system which is horizontally
> self-consistent and which vertically fits the facts?
> . . . Is not any hypothesis verifies when it brings
> meaning and order to those facts which are under
> study? . . . . The proof of an hypothesis is its
> ability to support a consistent world-view.[16]

The presuppositionalist method used by Carnell as a valid

means of verifying Christianity is by no means new to the

Christian tradition, although it has been often misinter-

preted.[17] Many leading thinkers in the Christian tradition

have worked with a similar methodology.

For instance, Augustine worked with faith as an as-

sumption. His famous dictum, "I believe in order that I may

know," pointed out his understanding of faith as an assumption

with which one works. But faith does not disavow reason; it

depends on reason for verification. Bernard Ramm says that,

for Augustine,

> constructive thought is possible only on a faith
> basis, viz, that we grant provisional status or
> truthfulness to propositions. A reason can only
> operate when interested and faith gives reason its
> interest and direction. But upon examination
> reason may then justly reject or accept what faith
> proposes . . . faith is grounded, is tested, is
> verified, and verified testimony attains to a
> state of being free from doubt.[18]

The man to whom Carnell was most indebted in his early

work was his former philosophy professor, Gordon Clark. Clark

defended presuppositionalism as a method which was not only

acceptable but necessary:

All thought depends on original assumptions. Just
as the theorems of geometry are deduced from the
axioms, so the conclusions of behaviorism are deduced from the assumption that mind is a physio-
logical process.[19]

Admittedly, original assumptions cannot be proved.

But what about these assumptions or axioms? Can
they be proved? It would seem that they cannot,
for they are the starting points of an argument,
and if the argument starts with them, there is
no preceding argumentation.[20]

To say, however, that original assumptions cannot be

proved does not mean that one can take comfort in skepticism:

Unfortunately, most unfortunately, even the comfort
of despair is not permitted the weary thinker, for,
even if nothing else can be demonstrated, the
falsity of skepticism can. Skepticism is the position that nothing can be demonstrated. And how,
we ask, can you demonstrate that nothing can be
demonstrated. The skeptic asserts that nothing
can be known. In his haste he said that truth was
impossible? For, if no proposition is true, then
at least one proposition is true--the proposition,
namely, that no proposition is true. If truth is
impossible, therefore, it follows that we have
already attained it. . . . Skepticism refutes itself because it is internally false. And when a
more elaborate complex of ideas is internally inconsistent, the complex must be rejected.[21]

Thus, it is evident that the presuppositionalist method

does not allow for internal self-contradiction or paradox.

Verification of any assumption must be on the basis of syste-

matic consistency. Any system, whether it be the absolute

idealism of Hegel, the dialectical materialism of Marx, the

systems of Berkeley and Bergson, or Christianity--any system

must show itself capable of consistency. Since there can only

be one self-consistent assumption or theory, if the test for the absence of truth is the law of contradiction, it naturally

follows that one can apply the law of contradiction to any

world-view, because the falsity of any theory will be estab-

lished if it is pursued long enough. As Clark states, "A

reductio ad absurdum would be the test."[22]

The method followed by Clark and Carnell is admittedly

open to problems. Clark was more specific in talking about

the difficulties than Carnell.[23] Since one must reduce to

absurdity all contending world-views, how can such an enormous

task be completed in one short lifetime? How can one who is

not omniscient apply the consistency test to the point of

total satisfaction? What if there are two or more fairly

self-consistent but mutually incompatible systems of thought?

Can one not simply suspend judgment without making a choice?

Neither Clark nor Carnell implied that their method is without

difficulty. Any method or any assumption will carry its own

problems. The point made by Clark is that there is enough

contrast between Christianity and other world-views, though

some systems of thought may as yet be large and incomplete,

that one must and can choose.[24]

> Our preferences, our standard of morality, our
> purpose in life accord with a theistic world-
> view or they do not. And if they do not, we
> are acting on the assumption, whether we admit
> it or not, that there is no God to hold us
> responsible. Suspension of judgment, so called,
> is but a disguised, if dignified, form of un-
> belief. A choice therefore cannot be avoided.[25]

The presupposition does not have to be free from dif-

ficulty to qualify as a viable option, but it must be internally consistent and must adequately answer to the practical and

theoretical predicament to be worthy of choice. Clark

stated:

> No philosopher is perfect and no system can
> give man omniscience. But if one system can
> provide plausible solutions to many problems
> while another leaves too many questions un-
> answered, if one system tends less to skepti-
> cism and gives more meaning to life, if one
> world-view is consistent while others are self-
> contradictory, who can deny us, since we must
> choose, the right to choose the more promising
> first principle.[26]

Despite the anti-metaphysical mood of modern empiricism,

Carnell believed that one could never solve the problem of

the one-within-the-many without resorting to the assumption

of supernatural revelation.[27] In fact, many leading evangel-

ical thinkers seem convinced that

> the frustration and pessimism which mark modern
> man's present mood must be preceded by a recapture
> of certain controlling ideas . . . . There must
> be restored to both philosophy and science a
> revelatory context.[28]

The Kantian prejudice failed to impress Carnell; he rejected

the modern assumption that "a rational man can no longer

believe in a supernaturally ordered world"[29] and accepted

Christianity which purports "to solve the basic problems

of epistemology and metaphysics, and to outline the nature

and destiny of man."[30] He wrote:

> Christianity assumes the existence of the God Who
> has revealed Himself in Scripture to solve both
> metaphysical and epistemological problems. With
> this postulate (the philosopher) can explain, not
> deny, experience. His major premise is no more
> ostentatious than of those who deny the existence
> of God as a condition sine qua non for interpreting
> reality.[31]

Concept of Truth

One of the basic concepts in Carnell's thought is that
of truth. It is this category that gives meaning to "good"
or "bad" judgments. Carnell defined truth as "correspondence
with the mind of God."[32] He further stated:

> On any level of judgment, therefore, man has truth
> only as long as he says about facts what God says
> about these facts. If man says that his chief
> end is to eat, drink, and be merry, he tells the
> truth only if that is what God says is man's chief
> end, too.[33]

Thus, the criterion of truth is being consistent with the
Author of all facts and meaning whose truth is to be found
in all verified fact and experience. The Scriptures are,
for Carnell, the best reflection of the mind of God, since
they have outlined a system of meaning which is internally
consistent.[34] The basic assumption that Carnell worked with
is that there is a consistency at work in the universe, the
ultimate source of which is God. "By consistency we mean
obedience to the law of contradiction. In any judgment a
term must mean one thing at a time if it is to convey truth."[35]
Contradiction means that truth is absent.

> Negatively, systematic consistency is true because
> it does not violate the law of contradiction . . . .
> Affirmatively, systematic consistency is marked
> by a devotion to all the facts of experience, for
> it is they that make up the content of our knowledge.
> The real is whatever we experience.[36]

Carnell believed that Edgar Sheffield Brightman, his former
professor at Boston University, was right when he concluded
that the test for truth must be based on total consistency

and not a spurious sensationalism or an empirically based

epistemology incapable of verification. For this reason,

Carnell rejected such epistemological judgments as instinct,

custom, tradition, consensus Gentium, feeling, sense per-

ception, intuition, correspondence, and pragmatism as valid

tests for truth.[37] After examining alternative bases of truth

Carnell concluded that systematic consistency is the only

criterion whereby one can know that his propositions are

true. Hence, total consistency means that propositions must

make peace with both logic and experience:

> A judgment is true and may be trusted when it
> sticks together with all of the facts of our
> experience, while a judgment is false when it
> cannot . . . . By 'experience' we mean that
> total breadth of human consciousness which
> embraces the entire rational, volitional, and
> emotional life of man, both within and without
> . . . . It is this breadth of definition which
> saves the Christian from the narrowness of
> either Spinozistic empiricism on the one hand
> or Humean empiricism on the other.[38]

When Carnell spoke of the law of contradiction he meant

that, A is not non-A. To agree to mutually contradictory

statements is to destroy all meaning in the word "rational."

Further, Carnell has characterized consistency by its

ability to account for all the facts of experience, not just

the logical. The law of contradiction does not demand that

one be able to see or understand all rational connections

in reality before affirming such reality--only that "one

cannot deny and affirm the same thing at the same time."[39]

While one may be unable to find meaning and coherence in the

empirical facts of life, special revelation (Bible) assures

the believer that a consistent teleological purpose exists.

Among the communicable attributes which God shares
with man, rationality is the one that directs man in his
search for truth. The _Imago Dei_ gives man the lucidity,
clarity, and rationality of thought that allows him to test
for truth. Man can test the Scriptures as well as his own
factual experiences to see if they are consistent with truth
(the mind of God):[40]

> Contrary to the hypothesis of some, the Bible is
> not an account of the religious experiences of
> men in given ages. Rather, it is 'the revelation
> of the mystery which was kept secret for long ages
> but is now disclosed and through the prophetic
> writings is made known to all nations, according
> to the command of the eternal God, to bring about
> obedience to the faith' (Romans 16:25-26). The
> Bible, since it contains a system of meaning which
> is systematically consistent, is a reflection of
> the mind of Christ. Knowing this corpus of reve-
> lation, through the witness of the Spirit in our
> hearts, we can say with Paul, 'we have the mind
> of Christ' (I Cor. 2:16). The mind of Christ is
> truth; we see it in God's revelation of word and
> fact. Soul-sorrow is cured by our seeing and
> embracing this truth. 'If you continue in my
> word, you are my disciples, and you will know the
> truth, and the truth will make you free' (John 8:32).[41]

Carnell's test for truth was, in reality, a curious inter-
larding of the criteria provided by Clark's dogmatism (Scripture
which is self-authenticating through the work of the Holy
Spirit but which is nonetheless, when tested, found to be
consistent) and Brightman's empirical coherence theory (a
reckoning with the total facts of experience which includes
consistency).[42]

This strange admixture of epistemologies which was
forged by Carnell's fertile mind into a synoptic criterion
for truth which he called "systematic consistency" tended
to take Carnell out of the good graces of his former mentors
Gordon Clark and Cornelius 'Van Til who were committed to
more closed systems of thought. Both of these men were
anti-empirical with regard to testing revelation, and they
were not much friendlier to a priori principles except for
the fact that they saw (particularly Clark) important
similarities between rationalism and biblical dogmatism.
The similarities consist in the fact that both posit a first
principle which is not demonstrable, and both are forms of
epistemological realism. Clark explains the first similarity:

> Dogmatism like rationalism posits a first princi-
> ple . . . .
> There must be principles. A system cannot start
> unless it starts. Therefore no one, since all
> must start somewhere, can consistently refuse
> permission to the dogmatist to start where he
> chooses.
> Yet there is great opposition to this, when it
> is a Christian dogmatist that claims the privi-
> lege . . . . Everyone except the skeptic is an
> authoritarian. Even the least knowledge depends
> on a first principle.[43]

Clark explains the second important similarity which
provides a philosophical basis for the memory and communicatic
of truth as well as a basis for belief in revelation as intellectual content or propositional truth. This view makes
revelation an experience of God's knowledge (the view held by
most fundamentalists) rather than an experience of the power

and active purpose of God (a view held by many devotees
of modernism and neo-orthodoxy).[44]

> . . . rationalism and dogmatism are forms of
> realism. Their epistemology is not repre-
> sentational.
>
> Christian dogmatism . . . must be realistic.
> The real object of knowledge is itself present
> to the mind. One need not (one cannot) pass
> from an image to the truth. One knows the
> truth itself. The real object is not momentary.
> It is not something that cannot return. Sen-
> sations exist only once. When my headache no
> longer aches and when I no longer see blue or
> taste sweet, the aches and the sweet simply do
> not exist . . . . An individual sensation never
> occurs again. But a truth is not a sensation.
> It returns and I can think it again many times.
> Not only so, but you can have it too.
> These objects of knowledge are not trivialities
> such as blues and sweets. They are truths or
> propositions. An example, one of these realities,
> a constituent of the noumenal world, is the
> proposition that God justifies sinners on the
> basis of Christ's imputed righteousness. This
> is a thought you and I can have simultaneously.
> Thus communication as well as memory is possible.
> There are of course other thoughts, objects, or
> realities. Every Biblical proposition is one.
> These never change nor go out of existence, for
> they are constituents of God's mind. Knowing
> them we know God.[45]

There is still, of course, the matter of the acceptance
of biblical revelation as true revelation. How can one prove
that the Bible is a divine revelation? The point is, according
to Clark, you cannot prove it; a dogmatist does not try to
prove it because it is a first principle which is not demonstrable.

Granted then that acceptance of biblical revelation is
a first indemonstrable principle, a second question is in
order: since the fact of life commits one to choose, how
does one decide between two incompatible first principles?

We noted earlier that Clark insists that a consistent

system is always preferable to self-contradictory ones,

but this is not the bed-rock reason why one can have faith

in the God of the Bible. Clark gave the answer which he

believed to be consistent with his first principle:

> Since all possible knowledge must be contained
> within the system and deduced from its first
> principles, the dogmatic answer must be found
> in the Bible itself. The answer is that faith
> is the gift of God.
>
> In evangelistic work there can be no appeal to
> secular, non-Christian material. There is an
> appeal -- it is the appeal of prayer to the Holy
> Spirit to cause the sinner to accept the truths
> of the gospel. Any other appeal is useless.
> If now a person wants the basic answer to the
> question, why does one man accept the Koran and
> another the Bible, this is it. God causes the
> one to believe.[46]

The dogmatist is not opposed to the use of empirical

data (historical evidence, archaeological data, etc.) or

the test for consistency as ad hominem arguments for what

they are worth (i.e., embarrassment for their adversaries),[47]

but he insists that neither the inductivist nor the a priori

reasoner can test the ultimate truth of revelation by anything

or any principle apart from the revelation itself. Along with

classical apologists Thomas Aquinas and William Paley and

various sorts of theological liberals, Clark categorized

Carnell, J. Oliver Buswell, John H. Gerstner, Floyd E. Hamilton

Arthur F. Holmes, George I. Mavrodes, and John Warick Montgomer

as evangelicals who had capitulated to empiricism.[48]

The position of Cornelius Van Til closely parallels that

of Clark. In his well-known work, The Defense of the Faith,

Van Til indirectly criticized Carnell's appeal to systematic consistency from the perspective of a staunch Calvinist. He wrote:

> . . . usually the traditional apologist is neither a pure inductivist nor a pure a priorist. Of necessity he has to be both. When engaged in inductive argument about facts he will therefore talk about these facts as proving the existence of God. If anything exists at all, he will say, something absolute must exist. But when he thus talks about what must exist and when he refuses even to admit that non-believers have false assumptions about their musts, let alone being willing to challenge them on the subject, he has in reality granted that the non-believer's conception about the relation of human logic to facts is correct. It does not occur to him that on any but the Christian theistic basis there is no possible connection of logic with facts at all. When the non-Christian, not working on the foundation of creation and providence, talks about musts in relation to facts he is beating the air. His logic is merely the exercise of a revolving door in a void, moving nothing from nowhere into the void. But instead of pointing out this fact to the unbeliever the traditional apologist appeals to this non-believer as though by his immanentistic method he could very well interpret many things correctly.[49]

Carnell respected Van Til's attempt to "bring the whole individual under captivity to God,"[50] but he denied his supposition that Calvinism is a perfectly true interpretation of Christian revelation as well as Van Til's rejection of "levels of truth" outside the Bible. In a stinging but respectful comeback at his former teacher, Carnell challenged Van Til on these two points. He commented that

> Apologists have usually tried to prove that unbelievers are already committed to truths which either rest on Christian foundations or, if held consistently, lead to conclusions which imply Christianity's antecedent truth.

. . . Dr. Van Til has greatly oversimplified
the problem of apologetics by his greatly over-
simplified view of the perfection of Calvinism.
His confidence that his own view cannot possibly
be wrong comforts him with the assurance that
other views cannot possibly be right.
Dr. Van Til is anxious to negate truth in unbelievers in order that Christianity's reality
may appear in absolute contrast. The fear is
that if unbelievers have any truth, Christianity
will only be 'better' than non-Christianity --
a matter of degrees in which absoluteness is
destroyed . . . . 'Preferable in regard to
value' says nothing about the degree to which
something is better. The difference can be
either relative of absolute. Once this clarification is made, we can defend levels of truth
in unbelievers without endangering the absoluteness of Christianity . . . if Dr. Van Til were
to inject this corrective into his system, he
would no longer believe that the main work of an
apologist consists in the negative task of refuting critics and attacking unbelievers.[51]

The Christian does not pit the gospel against culture;

by the wisdom received through Christian revelation he can

complete what is valid in the wisdom of the ages. "May the

sad day never come," Carnell said,"when Christians no longer

look for truth in Pericles' Funeral Oration of Mill's 'Essay

on Liberty.'"[52] The task of the apologist is to challenge the

unbeliever through a point of contact and remove any props

which may be serving to support his unbelief. He does not

seek to offend the truth which the unbeliever already possesse

Bernard Ramm has succinctly summarized Carnell's

epistemological position:

By the combination of a test for truth (systematic
consistency) and the data of Christianity (Bible),
the nature of man (Image of God), and the work of
the Spirit, we see how a man becomes a Christian
and having become one is convinced in mind as well
as in heart.[53]

It is noteworthy that Carnell was also critical of

Liberalism and Neo-orthodoxy on the problem of epistemology.

By making "feeling" the epistemological corridor to God,

modernism, he felt, was left with a subjectivism that could

not be tested:

> If feeling is the test of religious truth, how can
> one draw the line between valid and invalid religious
> feeling? . . . The obvious difficulty with modern-
> ism's theory of knowledge was that it could not be
> tested for error. This is fatal for any epistemology.
> When a man cannot test a system for error, he cannot
> validate it, for he never knows but that his very
> claim to truth might be an instance of the error
> which his methods cannot test.[54]

Replacing "feeling" with the "crisis" experience, Neo-

orthodoxy set out with scalpel in hand to dissect salvation

history (Heilsgeschichte) in the Bible from the ordinary his-

tory of blood, sweat, and tears.[55] In doing so, Carnell felt

that the Neo-orthodox thinkers had also lost the ability to

test for the truth of salvation:

> Nowhere does the Bible distinguish between ordinary
> and salvation history. . . . Neo-orthodoxy, however,
> is trying to perform surgery on the cancer or ordi-
> nary history and science. . . . The doctrinal claim
> of the writers of the Bible is that they are telling
> the mind of God wherever they speak. And if this
> doctrine is wrong, why should their doctrine suddenly
> be right when they begin to speak about salvation-
> history? . . . The Apostle Paul was willing to throw
> Christianity away entirely if Christ was not bodily
> raised from the grave (I Cor. 15:14). Yet Niebuhr
> calls the resurrection a 'myth' contending that
> salvation-history does not depend on the literal
> fact of the resurrection. . . . If faith and dog-
> matics have no part with philosophy and rational
> proof . . . the heart is bequeathed a bifurcation
> in knowledge which renders the conventional laws
> of philosophy impotent to test for the truth of
> revelation.[56]

That the rationalism of Carnell rebelled against the
subjective claims of liberalism and Neo-orthodoxy becomes
understandable when one recognizes that Carnell used "truth"
as a rationalistic epistemological category. Carnell wanted
to do what those in the subjective tradition of Søren
Kierkegaard said was impossible; he wanted to test truth against
experience, history, and science as well as for internal consistency. For Carnell, knowledge is never bifurcated; it
stands before the bar of verification in every area of life.

Concept of Faith

Carnell disavowed any definition of faith which separates
faith from the apprehension of truth. Faith is grounded in
knowledge and truth:

> Surely, if faith is not related to knowledge and
> truth, it is meaningless. It is more ouija-board
> than science. The Christian religion is indeed
> based on the act of faith, but faith that is not
> grounded in knowledge is but respectable(?) super-
> stition.[57]

Carnell did not say that evidences must precede faith,
but rather that faith must be open to what he called "internal"
and "external" facts. Since Carnell was satisfied that the
Bible meets the criterion of systematic consistency he was
willing to test all faith according to the canon of Scripture.
It is "externally" convincing: "Faith is but a whole-soul
trust in God's Word as true. When God says something, it is
true, for God cannot lie; and when man reposes in God's Word,
he has faith."[58]

But Carnell admitted that there were non-apologetic as well
as apologetic minds. Some men accept Christianity by an
intuitive grasp, never demanding the sufficiency of evidence.
For those more rational souls who must find rational verification to complement the internal experience of faith, Carnell
contended that it was available. There is a sufficiency of
internal evidence:

> The surest proof that one can have that his faith
> in God's Word is valid is the internal witness of
> the Spirit of God in his heart.
>
> . . . .
> God alone is a sufficient witness of Himself in his
> own word, so also the word will never gain credit
> in the hearts of men, till it be confirmed by the
> internal witness of the Spirit.[59]

Carnell did not seek to rob the Christian experience of
its "wisdom and power" by advocating a kind of biblicism that
"changes belief from repentence and commitment to the mere
acceptance of historical propositions."[60] Nor did he mean to
say that one can always understand the "whys" and "hows" of
God's dealings with man. The Spirit of God is not bound by
necessity but works according to the plan of God, outlined in
Holy writ. And the Spirit of God does not operate inconsistently
with the revealed mind of God: "Logic can be the means by
which the Spirit leads a man into faith, but it is the Spirit,
not logic, which finally seals the faith to the heart."[61]

Subjectivity is important in the Christian experience,
but it must be measured against the "solid rock of objective
truth . . . proper feeling, like proper mysticism, follows
upon the establishment of the truth of the law of God.

Truth establishes feelings; feelings do not establish truth."

Carnell rejected any kind of faith divorced from the law
of contradiction. Any dichotomy between faith and reason
leads to falsity. What appears to be "irrational" in the
major Christian doctrines is usually nothing more than the
assertion that these doctrines are distasteful to the objecto
According to Clark, the accusation is usually "not a substant
ated intellectual conclusion but an emotional antipathy.[64]
By denying reason, by disregarding the chief law of logic,
namely, the law of contradiction, one empties conversation
or argument of all meaning.

Perhaps one can best understand the categories of rationalists like Clark and Carnell by comparing them with men of a
more existential persuasion. For instance, Kierkegaard, in
the Concluding Unscientific Postscript declared that it makes
no difference whether a man prays to God or to an idol, provided he prays passionately:

> Truth, for Kierkegaard, lay in the inward How,
> not in the external What. If only the How of
> the individual is in truth, then the individual
> is in truth, even though he is related to untruth.[65]

The God-Man exists only for faith, not for verification by the
law of contradiction of any other law. The category of faith,
like the category of truth, is inward, subjective, and not
related to the rationalistic concept of truth as consistency
nor related to knowledge. While Clark and Carnell used faith
as an epistemological category, Kierkegaard did not. Faith fc

Kierkegaard was "that choice which a man makes when he encounters the truth as being--incarnated truth, primarily in
Christ, but also in every Christian--by which choice he
begins to become that truth himself, in his life."[66] One can
never verify the God-Man; one can only experience Him inwardly.
We can never understand nor subject the Absolute to the criterion of logic in His dealing with mankind. For man to sup-
-pose that his capacity to reason draws its ability from an
analogous fountainhead and to condition the unconditional to
such a restriction was, for Kierkegaard, absurd:

> If we could understand everything, we would in fact
> be God. But because we are not God, or rather be-
> cause God exists over against us as the Absolute,
> there can be no reason outside Himself for Him or
> for our belief in Him. Søren Kierkegaard is not
> advocating irrationality for there is 'faith's
> capacity to understand,' but rather a kind of
> commitment that transcends every category of knowl-
> edge and understanding: faith.[67]

Kierkegaard separated personal truth and philosophical
(logical) truth, but Clark and Carnell believed that there
was a monistic rational revelation of truth on which to build
faith. Clark referred to a "rational" revelation as one that
preserves the distinction between truth and falsity. "It is
in its entirety self-consistent. In other words, reason is
identified as the law of logic."[68] Clark condemned the concept of "truth," suggested by Emil Brunner, which cannot be
expressed in words or grasped in intellectual concepts.
Brunner had said:

> What this truth is, no one can say. Second, the
> words, sentences, and intellectual content that
> 'point to' this hidden truth may or may not be
> true. God can reveal himself (Wahrheit als Be-
> gegnung, p. 88) through false propositions as well
> as through true ones. We can never be sure, there-
> fore, that what God tells us is true. Falsehood
> and truth have equal value.[69]

It is obvious that the problematics of antithesis are not the

same when one examines the thought of men like Carnell and

Clark against men like Kierkegaard and Brunner. And these

varied concepts of "truth" give different bases for building

categories of ethics. For Clark and Carnell the antithesis

of truth is falsity. Falsity can be established when there

is a discrepancy between what the subject says is true and

what the objectively revealed Scriptures say is true:

> Since the mind of God perfectly knows reality, truth
> is property of that judgment which coincides with the
> mind of God. If man, thus, fails to say about reality
> what God says about it, he has made an error: for God,
> the source and power of all proper meaning and fact,
> cannot err in His judgment. Truth for the Christian,
> then, is defined as correspondence with the mind of God.[7]

Contrast this with the thinking of Kierkegaard who said that

there is no antithesis of truth per se. Truth is personal

by nature. It is subjective; one does not possess truth by

knowing, but rather he knows by doing:

> Indeed, properly speaking, one cannot know the
> truth; for if one knows the truth, he must know
> that to be the truth is the truth, and so in his
> knowledge of the truth he knows that this thing
> of knowing the truth is an untruth.[71]

Truth, according to Kierkegaard, is relative to the person.

Any category of ethics must be related to the person as he

finds himself in his particular situation, not to an inflexibl

principle or a canon of timeless "facts."

Faith, then, by its very nature, involves a risk.
The purpose of Christianity is not to impart knowledge but
to effect an "existential communication."[72] The supreme
example of faith is Abraham, offering up Isaac, in whom
Kierkegaard "sees the crowning proof that faith is wholly
opaque and irrational--something given, something done to us,
by which our whole being is convulsed."[73] The very antithesis of faith is sin.

Contrast this concept of faith with Carnell's. For
Carnell, faith is good faith when it is verifiable and can
be related to fact. Faith is bad faith when it does not
correspond to the depository of systematic consistency found
in special revelation; namely, the canon of Holy Scriptures.
Carnell believed that when one substituted any kind of
"inwardness" for the biblical criterion, he was opening the
door for unknowables which could never be verified as com-
prising true reality. It was on this score that the early
Carnell found himself at odds with theologians of "feeling"
like Kant, Ritschl. Schliermacher, and with later theologians
of "crisis" like Kierkegaard, Barth, and Brunner.

The Image of God

The category of the _Imago Dei_ was important for Carnell.
It is here that one can observe rationalism coming into full
bloom in his thinking. As Carnell noted before, it is the
Imago Dei that makes us rational creatures and "provides the

univocal point of meeting between God and man."[74] An es-

sential part of the nature of man is the capacity for

rationality which the Imago Dei provides. One might say that

man has the "ability to think God's thoughts after Him."[75]

This category helps us to understand what the Imago Dei es-

tablishes between God and man and how this view is opposed

to the whole empirical tradition in western civilization as

propounded by Locke, Hume, and others. Like empiricism,

rationalism has had a long standing tradition. The position

taken by Carnell was simply that man possesses "some" knowledg

which is not and cannot be derived through sense experience.

Plato talked about the forms, Augustine about the eternal

ideas. But in both cases the concepts or categories, in

terms of which man organizes his experiences are a priori;

that is, they are in some sense innate. As Carnell stated it,

"the Christian argues for the innate knowledge of logical

consistency as the basis for truth."[76] It is this form of

epistemology which makes the flux of history and of sensory

experience intelligible.

In An Introduction to Christian Apologetics Carnell buil

on this view to explain man's knowledge of God. The empirical

proofs for God's existence are invalid.[77] Instead, it is

the innate knowledge of logical consistency which provides

a criterion for truth, goodness, and beauty. To best under-

stand the issue between rationalism and empiricism, note what

Carnell meant by Christian rationalism:

We do not mean the ideal of classical rationalism,
as in Descartes, for example; namely, that all
knowledge is the same throughout and consists solely
in combining what is self-evident.
. . . .
According to Christian rationalism, however,
a "part" of our knowledge can be learned by such
anticipation. Since every human being is born with
a priori equipment as part of the image of God--an
endowment which belongs to man qua man-- our first
acts of knowledge in nature are possible because
we already know truths prior to sense experience.
Christian empiricism denies this, contending that
man must learn his first truths through sense
experience.

This is the crux: Christian rationalism accepts
the presupposition that the image of God in man
means at least that we are born with a clear knowledge
of God and of His law. Rather than building up a
knowledge of God through a patient examination of
the content of sense experience, we proceed to such
experience equipped with an awareness of God.[78]

Following the a priori method one finds a unifying

category that could never be found by the empirical method.

By starting with God one finds the One among the many. On

the other hand, by starting with the empirical many one can

never find the unifying One. For, as Carnell said, "From flux

only flux can come."[79]

Carnell readily admitted that all men begin knowing by

experiencing. Beyond one's natural environmental conditioning,[80]

which is common to all men, there are at least three starting

points which one can follow in trying to make ultimate "sense"

out of experience: "As we conceive it, there are three syn-

optic starting points--internal ineffable experience, internal

effable experience, and external effable experience."[81]

Because Carnell regarded truth as systematic consistency,

and believed that truth is capable of being expressed in com-

.

municable propositions, he rejected internal ineffable experience as a synoptic starting point because of its mystical
and irrational nature. Effable external experience is what
is generally known as empiricism. As we have already seen,
Carnell was critical of an epistemology built only from sense
experience, and he spent the better part of two chapters in
his first apologetical work refuting empiricism's epistemology
He criticized the famous "five proofs" individually and empiricism in general on the grounds that it could never solve
the theoretical human problem of the one-within-the-many.
Gordon Clark's succinct summary of the major objections to
empiricism parallels Carnell's views:

> There are three chief objections to empiricism.
> First, the impossibility of discovering any 'neces-
> sary connection' between events or ideas (i.e.,
> the denial of causality) makes historical and
> scientific investigation futile. At best, knowledge
> could not extend beyond one's own present impres-
> sions and their traces in memory. Second, the dis-
> integration of 'the self' results in a world of
> perceptions that no percipient perceives. This
> in effect annihilates memory. Third and fundamental,
> empiricism makes use of space and time surreptitiously
> at the beginning of the learning process, while
> explicitly these concepts are learned only at the
> end.[82]

In summary, truth, for Carnell, is universal and necessary.[83] It could never be derived from the flux of sense
perception alone. Skepticism is the logical end of such a
starting point.[84] Empiricism can only perpetuate the long
line of metaphysical questions. The only synoptic starting
point capable of satisfactorily answering to the human predicament is that of internal effable experience.

Carnell asserted that the implanted Imago Dei gives
every man certain categories (ideas) which establish an
innate criterion of knowledge. From the creator man enjoys
by natural endowment an "immediate apprehension of those
standards which make our search for the true, the good, and
the beautiful, meaningful."[85] This is not to say that all
experience in the soul is capable of being expressed, but
that "through a search of the soul's resident abilities universal and necessary principles, which are independent of
sense perception, can be located and plotted."[86]

As noted earlier, Christian rationalism is not new in
the tradition of western thought. Augustinian thought,
mediated through Descartes, reflects this kind of thinking.
Descartes asserted cogito, ergo sum--I think, therefore I am.
The appeal to the cogito, the knowledge of God from the self,
has traditionally been a rationalistic argument for the existence of God. Augustine and Descartes used it to refute
the skeptics of their day. Concerning the arguments validity,
Carnell said:

> The cogito establishes four things. First, it
> succeeds in drawing our attention from sensation-
> alism to the mind, the source of knowledge to
> which rationalists appeal. . . . Secondly, it
> is a rebuttal to all who say that there is nothing
> in the intellect which was not previously in the
> senses. . . . Thirdly, the cogito provides us
> with a knowledge of God. Knowing what truth is,
> we know what God is, for God is truth. . . .
> Fourthly, the cogito allows us to make univocal
> predictions about God, for we are not limited in
> our rationes to those which can be abstracted from
> sensation. In properly knowing ourselves, we know
> truth; and God is truth.[87]

Enlarging on the Augustinian argument, John Calvin
insisted that we can know more than our own existence; we
can possess some knowledge of God by reason of our knowledge
of ourselves. Using the argument of Calvin, Carnell asserted that "without the aid of sensation, man knows that
he is finite, dependent, and wretched."[88] We already know,
at least in part, what certain theological categories
(creation, fall, judgment, etc.) mean by reason of our own
finitude and dependence. The sensus divinitatis beckons us
to look beyond ourselves to God and His perfection.

The innate quality separating truth from falsity in
sense perception is the law of contradiction. Reason must
balk at paradox and its claims that something can be, at
one and the same time, the antithesis of itself.

Further, there is the innate quality allowing one to
distinguish between right and wrong (ethics). Carnell did
not mean by this that all men will conceive of the same
conduct as being good or bad, but rather that all men know
that there is a distinction between the good and the bad:

> Not all men may know how to apply their knowledge
> of right and wrong consistently, to be sure, but
> this does not destroy the criteria themselves.
> 'As thinkers may differ in their conclusions and
> all seek the truth in distinction from error, so
> in general ethical norms may differ, yet all seek
> the good in distinction from evil.'[89]

Aesthetically, there are the innate criteria that separate the "beautiful" from the "ugly." These criteria enable
one to say that "a Mozart quartet is better than a chorus of
cats" or that "the Golden Gate bridge is prettier than a

crushed cigar box."[90] Bernard Ramm has succinctly stated the

point concerning the idealism of Carnell:

> The most general affirmation underlying all three
> (logical, ethical, and aesthetical) is that mean-
> ingful experience and meaningful judgments in these
> three areas are impossible from the standpoint of
> a strict empiricism, but the very existence of
> logical, ethical, and aesthetic evaluations proves
> the existence of logical, ethical, and aesthetic
> ideas . . . . Relentlessly Carnell argues that
> in the fields of logic, ethics, and aesthetics
> chaos ensues if rationalistic premises are abandoned
> . . . . Irrational thought, immoral behavior, and
> ugly art have equal standing with rational thought,
> moral behavior, and beautiful art. But if mankind
> followed such a philosophy thoroughly, anarchy in
> all fields of human knowledge would result. Eternal
> concepts alone give intelligibility to logic, sub-
> stantiality to ethics, and fabric to aesthetics.[91]

To recapitulate, Carnell contended that God has made us

in his image which meant, for Carnell, that we are endowed

with rational natures which provide the univocal point of

meeting between God and man. This is not just an abstract

principle of rationality; it is reality ordered by the will

and pleasure of a personal God.[92] The implication of the

Imago Dei is that

> since every human being is born with a priori
> equipment as part of the image of God--an en-
> dowment which belongs to man qua man--our first
> acts of knowledge in nature are possible because
> we already know other truths prior to sense
> experience.[93]

This is denied by the empiricist who contends that man's

first truths are learned through sense experience.

Revelation

In turning to the category of revelation we come to

the heart of Carnell's thought in An Introduction to Christian

Apologetics. Like many previous theologians, Carnell categorized revelation under two headings: General revelation
and Special revelation.

In General revelation the handiwork of God in nature
"reminds" us of the God we already know from the innate
Imago Dei.[94] All men are blessed with what Kant called "the
starry heavens above him and the moral law within," but these
are, despite their reflectiveness, incapable of giving man
the more specific answers to the weighty questions of life
such as: "What is the nature of God? What is His relation
to the process of history? What is His relation to our
rationes? What must we do to be saved?"[95]

Special revelation, "the full and whole sixty-six canoni-
cal books which make up the Bible," is the only source that
can adequately answer to the human predicament. Scripture
alone furnishes the details of the theistic scheme which
gives meaning to the world as well as providing the means
for personal happiness, eternal life through the death and
resurrection of Jesus Christ.

Carnell's starting point in Special revelation was neces-
sitated by the lack of information in General revelation as
well as by the consequence of the Fall. For Thomas Aquinas
only the will, not the intellect, had been seriously damaged
by the Fall. The intellect became more autonomous; it was believed that "rational thought operating on the data provided by
the senses can reach theological conclusions which are called
natural theology."[96] But for Carnell, man needed Divine
revelation, such as he has in the Scriptures, to illuminate

a path which had been darkened by sin:

> The reason of man, in addition to being by nature
> corrupted by sin, is incompetent to work out a
> complete view of God and man because it, in its
> unaided state, is not supplied with enough in-
> formation to complete its philosophy. The data
> which special revelation supplies is needed to
> supplement the data which natural revelation
> displays.[97]

In making the transition from natural revelation to

Special revelation Carnell was not opting for a bifurcation

of knowledge. One does not deal with nature by reason and

the Scriptures by faith:

> We are not exchanging reason for faith, as did
> Thomas; rather we are seeking to strengthen the
> faith which we already have, for faith is a
> resting of the heart in the worthiness of the
> evidence. The Bible is needed to give us more
> evidence.[98]

The Scriptures must pass the same test as any other purported

truth, the test for systematic consistency. Thus, when one

retorts that there are many so-called revelations which seek

our acceptance, Carnell replies:

> Accept that revelation which, when examined, yields
> a system of thought which is horizontally self-
> consistent and which vertically fits the facts of
> history. . . . Bring on your revelations! Let them
> make peace with the law of contradiction and the
> facts of history, and they will deserve a rational
> man's assent. A careful examination of the Bible
> reveals that it passes these stringent examinations
> summa cum laude. Unlike all other religious volumes,
> the Bible speaks of, and gives a metaphysical basis
> to, the unity and solidarity of the entire human
> race under God. Christ's message has nothing clan-
> nish, tribal, esoteric, or racial about it. Christ
> was not only in sympathy with the building of a
> bridge of brotherhood that would wipe out all class
> distinctions, but He expressly lived and died to make
> all men one in Him by His cross. . . . He combines
> in Himself all of the best virtues of the East and the West.[99]

The _telos_ of God is not contrary to reason; it is within the law of contradiction. And the history of that _telos_ is no different than ordinary history. In disavowing any distinction between _Weltgeschichte_ and _Heilsgeschichte_, Carnell believed that Christianity should be historically verified in the same way as any other historical event.

It was admitted that there are many difficulties, not easily resolved, that one must face when he takes as his hypothesis "the God who has revealed Himself in Scripture." But there are difficulties with any hypothesis.[100] Carnell's purpose was not to find a perfect system of philosophy but to accept that system of thought which is most coherent, best fitting the test for truth.

To reiterate what was said earlier, Carnell used his analysis of the human predicament as a basis on which to build an apologetic. He desired to defend Christianity as a system of thought capable of adequately answering the questions implied in human existence. Theoretically, there is the problem of the one-within-the-many. Without a principle of unity there can be no rational explanation for reality. And, as Carnell stated it, "The task of any philosophy of life is to construct a rational explanation for the whole course of reality."[101] Practically, there is the problem of man living in history, yet transcending history, so that he can never be happy until he can successfully relate the real (empirical) and the ideal (rational) world. Carnell worked with the

assumption that "the God who had revealed Himself in Scripture"
is the unifying principle and that He alone can provide the
solution to man's problem of existence. And this He has done
in sacrificial love through the cross. With Christ, the
Logos, as the "synthesizing principle and the true meaning of
all reality"[102] one has a basis for truth and faith: "Truth
is propositional correspondence to God's mind and the test
for truth is systematic consistency."[103] When one, through
Special revelation, sees Christ as the cure for "soul-sorrow,"
one has a basis for truth and faith:

> When a man sees and embraces this truth with a
> cordial trust, he has proper faith, for generic
> faith is but a resting of the heart in the suf-
> ficiency of the evidence. . . . In possessing
> truth, the Christian possesses the Christ Himself.[104]

By appealing to Special revelation as his major epistemological premise, Carnell believed that one can appropriate the
facts of Special revelation to the fragmented knowledge that
he already has from the cogito, the finitude of the self, and
the rationes aeternae.[105]

More importantly, Special revelation reveals the personal,
compassionate love of God and the possibility of man's personal
encounter with God through trust.[106]

Further, Special revelation provides answers for the
broad theoretical problems that have always plagued mankind:

> When he appropriates the implications that are found
> in the Bible for life's meaning, the Christian solves
> the problem of common ground, the relation between
> science and theology, the problem of miracles, the

philosophy of history, the problem of evil, the
ethical one and many, and the hope of immortality
and the resurrection. Upon every important theoretical problem of life, the Bible has reliable,
logical judgments to offer, judgments which, when
accepted by the whole heart and soul, yield a system of thought which is horizontally self-consistent
and which vertically fits the facts of life.[107]

Carnell best stated his own case in his concluding remarks:

If a man rejects the solution to the riddle of the
universe that Christ offers, and if he cannot believe in a system of philosophy which at least
professes to answer the question of the rationality of the universe, to solve the dilemma of truth,
and to provide a basis for personal immortality,
how shall he answer Peter's question, 'to whom
shall we go?' (John 6:68)[108]

CHAPTER IV

CARNELL IN TRANSITION

If one's interest in Carnell should wane after a
reading of An Introduction to Christian Apologetics, one
could conclude that Carnell's approach to apologetics was
purely intellectual. Carnell would be thought of as an
apologist of the mind and not of the heart. His apologetic
would be considered one-sided, rather than directed toward
the total man.

To judge Carnell solely on the basis of his first
apologetical concern, however, is to prejudice one's opinion
too quickly. In this chapter the primary objective is to
examine Carnell's second major work, A Philosophy of the
Christian Religion. In this work one can observe a broadening
of Carnell's thought to include axiology, as well as some
subsequent significant shifts in thought. Like all rationalists,
Carnell leaned toward the view that a "proper perspective"
of man meant that one should first deal with matters of the
intellect. But Carnell was not purely a cartesian rationalist.
He was well aware that there were intangible, indefinable,
experiential realities of the heart[1] which defy all attempts
of consistency[2] and propositional explanation. Those realities

81

which men choose when seeking an increase in happiness are

known as values. Since, in the opinion of Carnell, one will

not choose a value by which to live and die until he is ration

ly convinced that it is meaningful and non-contradictory,

it seemed proper to him to deal first with matters of reason.

And in his shift to axiology Carnell never wavered from his

conviction that rationality was necessary and primary for

the apologist:

> No man can meaningfully deny the primacy of the
> laws of logic. Their universality and necessity
> are secured by the simple fact that nothing has
> significance apart from them. Men do not invent
> the fundamental laws of logic, for nothing would
> mean anything if logic did not first mean what it
> says. In the words of McTaggart, no man ever tried
> to break logic but what logic broke him. Even the
> man who tries to argue against the priority of
> logic must in his argument employ the very canons
> he is seeking to destroy. Using logic to disprove
> logic is as foolish as catching rapid breaths while
> preaching that it is not necessary to breathe.[3]

The Whole Man

To say that one should first be sure that what one chooses

is meaningful is not to say that a premium should be placed on

inferential thinking as an end in itself.[4] Man is not es-

sentially nous:

> The I is the whole person--intellect, emotions, will,
> etc. The I is the totality of all that is meant to
> be spirit and body compounded in personality. The
> individual is an organic whole, and thinking is one
> phase of his activities.[5]

Even in his complexity, however, man does not dichotomize.

He does not distinguish between intellect and emotions for they

are part of the whole man:

When the Scriptures interlard poetic insight with
formal, doctrinal consistency, therefore, it should
be observed that such a procedure is what we should
expect if the whole man is being addressed.[6]

In turning to axiology Carnell demonstrated his awareness

of the double environment in which man exists. Apart from

his ability to reason man knows, through heart knowledge,

"a depth of insight which, while it may never be separated

from rational consistency, is yet not univocally identified

with such consistency."[7] In the Apologetic Carnell acknowledged

the experiential, the emotional, and the aesthetical, but his

emphasis was on the ability of Christianity to satisfy the

rational demands of man. In the Philosophy inwardness became

the greater concern. As Ramm notes,

> In the Philosophy he (Carnell) has emphasized the place
> of the aesthetic in Christianity, i.e., its ability
> to satisfy man on the vital fringes of the mystical
> which gives life its color, dynamic and interest and
> relieves him of any charge of having a purely intel-
> lectualistic apologetic.[8]

In his broadening development Carnell made room for heart

knowledge, as well as "logical thought," so that truth is not

only systematic consistency or propositional correspondence

to reality; "truth is the sum total of reality itself."[9]

Taking his cue from Kierkegaard, Carnell acknowledged that

truth is more than comprehending; truth is "being."[10] As

Carnell explained,

> God has so tempered truth together that no locus
> may say to another, I have no need of you. Truth
> as reality makes up the environment for fellowship;
> truth as propositional correspondence to reality
> defines the criteria of true fellowship; while
> truth as goodness of character is the fellowship
> itself. These loci must act tunefully if the whole

man is to be harmoniously related both to the
universe over against him and to the totality
of his own person within.[11]

In acknowledging the environment of the heart Carnell

found it necessary to distinguish knowledge by inference

from what he called "knowledge by acquaintance."[12] Epistemo-

logically, knowledge by acquaintance is the highest form of

truth and the kind of truth which Biblical writers consistently

exhort one to enjoy. Here the emphasis is on "fellowship"

where spirit enters spirit in direct acquaintance:

> The apex in the pyramid of knowledge is personal
> acquaintance with God. When the creature finds
> his way to fellowship with God, the image and
> likeness returns to the center and source of its
> being, there to enjoy that perfection of love
> which human relations can enjoy only by finite
> degrees.[12]

> Human love opens the way to divine love; but once
> the divine love has been tasted, human love is then
> evaluated in the light of its perfection. There is
> no greater height of free potentiality, and thus
> no more conceivably perfect form of knowledge, than
> that enjoyed when the dust returns to the potter to
> experience fellowship and love.[13]

At this juncture one can see that Carnell is appealing

to a broader and higher principle of verification than he

had previously acknowledged. He called it the third locus

of truth, "truth in the heart." It is this kind of epistemology

that accounts for man's ability to enjoy person to person

fellowship. Indeed, this was a step in the direction of a

new emphasis on inwardness and subjectivity, though it was

never divorced from rational explication and objective grounding

Carnell had a certain admiration for Kierkegaard, es-

pecially in regard to his defense of the third locus of truth:
"Demanding that Christianity be interpreted as a living truth
rather than a system of thought, he (Kierkegaard) set a fresh
pace within the philosophy of religion."[15]

The strange Danish philosopher-theologian (1813-1855)
of the nineteenth century, is often acknowledged as the father
of modern existentialism. Kierkegaard revolted against the
abstract thought in the philosophy and religion of his day.
The purpose of religion, he said, is not to know dogmas or
ideas but to live them. As such, Kierkegaard insisted on
an emphasis upon man as an individual, considering the pos-
sibilities of human existence. The primary concern in
Christianity is not its contents but in "becoming a Christian."
What does becoming a Christian involve? It involves a leap
of faith, a radical commitment of one's whole life. God can
never be known by reason. In fact, when God is known he
appears paradoxical to our reason. God is known only as
he concretely makes himself known as a living factor in our
lives. When man reflects on his situation he is driven to
despair, and in his despair he is ready to grasp the salvation
that God offers to him. When one takes the ethical life
seriously, one is brought to despair by his own failure. But
in the leap of faith whereby one chooses to follow Christ,
there is a kind of moral certainty, though doubt is never
completely overcome. Kierkegaard did not pretend to offer
certainty, only a leap, a finding of one's self by willing

to lose it in Christ. Thus, the Christian life is not a life of indolent certainty and verification. It is a struggle to attain faith against despair and offense.

Kierkegaard's God is radically transcendent. Man is separated from God by his sin and guilt. Even in the leap of faith God must come to man. Man cannot lift himself to God. Like Luther, Kierkegaard was a theologian of grace.

Clearly, becoming a Christian, for Kierkegaard, did not mean believing doctrines or rationally understanding Christianity. It meant the continual giving of one's whole life. As has already been indicated, Carnell was highly influenced by this Danish theological gadfly, who sought to make Christianity what he felt it was meant to be, dynamic and demanding.

It must be pointed out, however, that Carnell was critical of Kierkegaard on several crucial issues and cannot be regarded as an existentialist in the Kierkegaardian sense, though his Philosophy did offer a fresh and welcomed emphasis on the inwardness of heart values. Without attempting to summarize completely Carnell's lengthy treatment of Kierkegaar it is important to detail the major differences. While Carnel was willing to glean all that he could from a "healthy" subjectivity, that is, self-transcendence in search of responsibl individuality, he was not convinced that inwardness is lost when the mind is satisfied with the consistency of objective evidences. On the contrary,

> it is not psychologically true that passionate
> concern increases in commensurate ratio to ob-
> jective uncertainty. In our daily living we

proportion our inward response to the certainty
of the evidences . . . . Thus, a faith based on
rational evidences is able to nourish a healthy
inwardness. . . . There is no convincing reason
why time-eternity relations should stand outside
of the conventional connections of rational coherence.[16]

The inevitable result of setting faith against logic

is a loss of a test for error, and Carnell was not ready to

concede that misplaced passion is more important than eternal

and objective truth.

Secondly, Carnell was distrustful of any attempt to

bifurcate knowledge so that a "leap of faith" becomes neces-

sary between the natural and the supernatural (temporal and

eternal). The result would be disastrous:

There is no way to safeguard theology or philosophy
as sciences apart from the presupposition that a
single genus of knowledge envelops both time and
eternity. If revelation is one type of knowledge
and science and philosophy another, a hopeless bifurcation results in which there remains no universal and necessary test for truth.[17]

The Imago Dei insures man's capacity for judgment by

giving him reason with which to judge contradiction. Jesus

Christ is worthy of our faith because "both his person and

his doctrine are rationally continuous with the values which

we have already accepted in ordinary experience."[18] There

is no need for a "leap." Whenever spirit is satisfied that

the evidences are sufficient, it rests in truth.

Carnell realized the vice as well as the virtue of

existentialism. While recognizing man's freedom and self-

transcendence he also believed it necessary for man to

understand something of essence as well as existence. Without

eternal and changeless criteria to define its limits, un-
bounded freedom can only lead to an absurd and nihilistic
view of life. This is essentially what has happened to
thinkers like Sartre, Heideg\`gar, and Camus who have sought
to find themselves by losing the reality that is over against
them. Carnell says:

> Existentialism forces us to be unnatural. Because
> freedom stands under the impulsion of rationes
> aeternae, we must discipline ourselves to reckon
> with those objective forms which define the limits
> of legitimate creativity. Freedom finds the values
> of truth, goodness, and beauty; it does not create
> them. Let creativity be infinite; but let it be
> infinite creativity. Without transtemporal, trans-
> spatial criteria to serve as guides in our freedom,
> we shall so obliterate the differences between cre-
> ative progress and destructive retrogression that
> all significance in life will be destroyed. Unless
> we are getting somewhere in our freedom, we are
> simply caught in the prison discipline of walking
> in a treadmill.[19]

The point to be made is that Carnell, like Kierkegaard,
stessed inwardness, passion, and subjectivity, but not at
the expense of placing the subjective and objective loci
of truth in opposing relations, the final result of which
would mean the destruction of the free individual himself.[20]
Axiologically, Christianity is a wise choice because it
can meet the needs of the whole man:

> Submission to the system of Biblical Christianity
> is good, not because complacency is destroyed by
> absurdities, but because the system is able to
> support spirituality through its rigorous syste-
> matic consistency. If a man seeks to increase
> inwardness, therefore, let him adorn, not belittle,
> that metaphysical system which alone makes being
> an individual--or anything else--meaningful.[21]

Wisdom

In An Introduction to Christian Apologetics Carnell
endeavored to demonstrate that Christianity is intellectually
consistent. In A Philosophy of the Christian Religion he
sought to establish the wisdom of choosing Christianity
axiologically. In Apologetics the unbeliever is shown to
be inconsistent, whereas in Philosophy he is shown to be foolish.
Bernard Ramm believes that Carnell's approach is broad enough
for the whole man. He says:

> These two books complement each other, the one
> having its appeal to the reader with the rational
> interests, and the other to those with the warmer
> interests of wholeness and heart. If the Apologetics
> is the eye, the Philosophy is the hand, and neither
> can say to the other that it has no use for it. Both
> structures are important.[22]

Wholeness is characterized by perspective. While all
men by nature[23] seek happiness, it is a fact that some seek
foolishly by making unwise decisions while others seek
wisely by making decisions that will not bring regret. Like
wholeness, wisdom is characterized by full perspective coherence; folly is known by its partiality. That is to say,
one is wise in his values when he chooses that which will
not bring regret in the end. To choose the immediate and
the partial is to misuse one's freedom. Carnell writes,
"Values are judged by their power to increase or decrease
happiness."[24] The Scriptures presuppose that a wise man will
choose that which will bring wholeness and happiness to both
the breadth and depth of life. "Wisdom looks to the ends."[25]

To ignore the ultimate consequences of one's values is to court disaster. Full perspective is the criterion by which to judge values. Men may talk of a "meaningless universe" and of "ultimate emptiness" but "our heart tells us that there are destinies at stake in this life."[26] At any rate, "living takes on dignity, faith, and hope when freedom is persuaded that it is truly dealing with ultimate reality."[27] It is the ultimate, the eternal, and the changeless which dignify our choice. When one chooses that which can only satisfy the immediate, the temporal, and the partial, one has chosen immediacy. While immediacy promises the gratification of instantaneity, accessibility, and intensity, man is always encouraged to expect more than is there. The pleasures of immediacy are real, but one has sacrificed the union of self with the eternal for the temporary pleasure of uniting self with the immediate. When one looks at life in its total perspective, one will choose that which will not ultimately bring regret. Regret results when the transcenden self is not allowed to guide the involved self toward satisfaction of the whole man. Since immediate pleasures can never satisify the whole man, it is unwise to choose pleasure as a value for which to live and die:

> Pleasure still lures men as the voice of the sirens near the Surrentine promontory lured Odysseus and his men. But the end of those who guide their ships toward it is yet destruction. The ship is the self and the destruction is the boredom of distaste and vapidness, the frustration of disappointment, the guilt of failure, and the exhaustion of weakness and despair.

Out of the involved dialogue between the self and
the pretensions of immediacy there emerges a rather
clear conclusion: "Final satisfaction is not here.
Seek it elsewhere." The answer is negative, but
unequivocal. Odysseus solved his problem by putting
wax in the ears of his sailors and lashing himself
to the ship. Perhaps the free self can solve the
matter by the expulsive power of a higher love.[28]

One of the most promising values of the twentieth century,

especially of the exploited classes, is materialism. Built

on the communistic ideology of Karl Marx, dialectical ma-

terialism has offered a materialistic world-view to millions

who have allied themselves in a struggle against social and

economic injustice. The hope of the communist is a "classless"

society where there will be bread for all, a society in which

every man can give according to his ability and receive ac-

cording to his need.

According to Carnell, however, materialism is only another

form of immediacy. Such a one-dimension view of man cannot

satisfy a creature whose freedom demands more than bread.

Communism operates on the standards of the body alone, leaving

the heart void of satisfaction. The spiritual is subordinated

and explained by the material.[29] Like hedonism, Marxism fails

to satisfy the free self with its ideal of the classless so-

ciety. "If the classless society is attained, then the indi-

vidual becomes bored. And if it is not attained, then the

individual is frustrated."[30] Further, whether the ideal is

or is not reached, the individual in such a society is only

happy if and when he is an active member of the party. When

the material fails, the spirit is impoverished. Reinhold

Niebuhr has observed that a materialistic ideology is successful because it appeals to man's inclinations, not to
his highest values. He says:

> The false prophet preaches security to those
> who make their own inclinations the law of
> life and who thereby despise and defy God.
> The prophecy is false because a life which
> defies the laws of life in order to gain se-
> curity destroys what it is seeking to establish.[31]

Carnell contends that the free self knows innately that
there is a higher commitment to be made; there is a normative
criterion of truth, goodness, and beauty independent of the
materialism of communism. Man's need for bread and material
good cannot be denied, nor should it be minimized, but any
anthropology with values which forfeit the dignity of man,
created in the image of God and endowed with the spiritual
quality of self-transcendence, destroys individuality and
is guilty of self-destruction.[32] Eternal potentialities
cannot be satisfied with immediate material possessions. Carn
attacked the discrepancy in this way:

> Communism opens wide its arms to solve the problem
> of injustice, but it does it at the cost of rejecting
> the very spiritual and moral vitalities by which all
> decency is preserved. This makes a Judas Iscariot
> of a communist. He prefers the bag instead of honesty,
> righteousness, justice, and love. He demands economic
> and social security at such a cost that in the end
> he is willing to betray his own friends for the sake
> of a few shekels. But when he comes to himself,
> frustrated over trying to unite spiritual freedom
> with material coins, the free self charges on the
> involved self; and the hangman's noose is the only
> way out. Marx has betrayed the normative rules of
> morality and justice with the sweet kiss of dialectical
> materialism. Under one arm he carries the bag, while
> under the other he carries a hangman's noose.

> Western culture is founded on the faith that there
> is an archetypical world of truth, goodness, and
> beauty which stands over history as its changeless
> norm. Plato called it the world of Ideas; Christi-
> anity calls it the mind of God. The just and the
> right are exemplified, not made, by the tensions
> of history.[33]

Carnell wrote A Philosophy of the Christian Religion

in 1952, when "cold war" attitudes were high and many times

over-exaggerated. The view can be justified that, in general,

Carnell has over simplified Marxian Communism. Further, it

would not be too difficult to demonstrate that capitalism

is often just as materialistic. But this is not the point.

The point that is meant to be made is that any kind of ma-

terialism is incapable of increasing the happiness of the

whole man. Therefore, materialism is not a wise choice when

one is selecting a value by which to live and die.

Speaking of yet another value, Carnell believed that

much of the problem with modern man's search for truth and

fulfillment lies in the fact that he is approaching it with

the wrong "method"; modern man labors under an epistemology

that is unable to explain or understand his double environment.

While methodology may seem like an unnatural category when

speaking of values, Carnell was convinced that it was not.

The method itself is a value. If one has unwisely chosen a

deficient method, or if one does not recognize the limitations

of his method, one may find that he is over-committed to a

value that cannot ultimately satisfy. Science and the scien-

tific method are values to which many have attached themselves;

in science one looks for a quantitative, measurable explanation of man. But even philosophers have become so enthralled with the method of science as to use it for purposes for which it does not qualify; namely, to measure the qualitative and the normative.[34]

Positivism, with its emphasis on precision, objectivity, and the unambiguous is a good example of a consistent a posteriori philosophy. In seeking to inquire into the limits and structure of meaningful discourse the positivist constructs a logic of language to attain assurance of significant communication. Because of the restrictions of his method he cannot pass from the descriptive to the normative. The qualitative is subjugated to the quantitative. The reality of such qualities as love, joy, hope, friendship, peace and faith are ruled out because they cannot be subjected to scientific analysis. There is a loss of metaphysical concern because cosmic values cannot be measured and are thus considered to be nonexistent.[35] Ethical propositions derived from metaphysical ultimates are dismissed because they cannot be reduced from the qualitative to the quantitative.[36] In short, the scientific method, when used to measure the qualitative and the normative, has resulted in a costly reduction. As Carnell observed,

> A new religion has started--worship of the scientific method. And the faith which binds the members of this cult together is the blinding creed that man was made for the scientific method and not the method for man.[38]

Man, however, cannot be understood nor explained from this over simplified view of reality:

> Man lives in a double environment. Conscience cries out against the possibility of man's being explained on a one-dimensional view of reality. His freedom is compounded with moral responsibility and moral responsibility proceeds from an eternal ought.[39]

The scientific method can be used to measure the quantitative but one would be foolish to live and die for a method that cannot account for the a priori realities of the heart:

> The heart refuses to be troubled any further by an offer to live and die for the scientific method. It is a pretty poor bargain when one trades everything in life that counts for the anemic gain of being able to classify sentences.
>
> Whoever continues to repeat the stupid claim that sentences about justice, honor, chastity, self-control, piety, holiness and love are non-cognitive, should be laughed at--laughed at good and hard. He shows not only a want of education, but also a want of common sense. There are standards so ultimate to all meaning that all else is judged by them. How then can they be judged a subordinate method? If science is not good, what is it good for? If science is not true, why should one believe it?[40]

In moving from one value option to another, Carnell observed that many have been prone to sacrifice the primacy of self-transcendent spirit for a knowledge of rational and natural connections. And in so doing, they have adopted the value of philosophical ataraxia; that is to say, there are those who seem to find contentment in knowing the rational and natural connections between things. Carnell observes:

> The greying geologist poring over a new specimen of rock stratum, the botanist engrossed in the examination of a fresh shipment of exotic plants, the patient physicist constructing a complicated apparatus for testing a new by-product of atomic power--all are convincing instances of the dynamic of the rational ideal.[41]

Carnell would readily agree that one cannot meaningfully deny the primacy of the laws of logic. For, as Carnell has continuously argued, the foundation of all meaning is the law of contradiction. But to find comfort and contentment in inferential knowledge as an ultimate value is an inferior mode of existence. The essential man is not the rational man Man is a whole person--intellect, emotions, will, etc. He is never fully satisfied with philosophical ataraxia; man is a free spirit and can only be satisfied when he is able to meet the needs of his person in "fellowship." The height of free potentiality is enjoyed when man returns to God to experience fellowship and love.[42] Love transcends immediacy and boredom. Knowledge by acquaintance is a higher epistemology than knowledge by inference. Wisdom dictates that both are necessary and good, but an increase in happiness can result only when one chooses the higher:

> All of the types of knowledge are appropriate for the office and object to which they are assigned. Epistemologically, God has tempered the faculties of knowledge together, giving abundant honor to that which seemingly lacks. Knowledge by inference, while a sine qua non for the perception of valid connections, is yet a handmaid to knowledge by acquaintance; for by inference we can only anticipate the perfection which we can enjoy immediately through experience. And acquaintance knowledge of things is a handmaid of acquaintance knowledge of persons, since the former contains only in type what the latter enjoys as fulfillment. To be acquainted with the hills of home is fine; to be acquainted with mother or father is more excellent.[43]

Wisdom, as an end in itself, can never satisfy the inner longings of the human heart. Wisdom, as a rational ideal,

is not a value worthy of one's ultimate devotion. Perfection in wisdom is reached when one enjoys fellowship and
communion, not when one is able only to perceive the rational
connections in a formal syllogism.[44]

Knowledge, by inference, is another form of immediacy,
and as such, it is unworthy of the free man's ultimate commitment. Since the whole man cannot be satisfied with rational knowledge alone, any value commitment to philosophical
ataraxia would prove finally dissatisfying. A wise man will
not be satisfied with less than the best when choosing a
value for which to live and die.

Humanism, with its devotion to the interests of human
beings, seems to many to be a logical choice. Humanism has
been and still remains a strong contender for supremacy in
modern man's structuring of values. By combining a good
method (scientific method) with good values (humanity) the
humanist seeks to satisfy the whole man (both head and heart).
He is interested in understanding and conserving human values;
it is the person of man that is important. Man is seen as
characterized by goodness and almost infinite possibility.
The task of man is first to realize his potential for self-
perfectibility and then to work toward the goals of individual
and social integration. Carnell thus described the humanist
attitude:

> Man is very much here, and it is the duty of both
> religion and science to find the causal connections
> which will prevent individuals from being frustrated
> either by the universe or by their relations to each
> other. . . . Instead of belittling himself as a
> chronic sinner, man must begin to realize his po-

tentialities for self-perfectibility.[45]

For the humanist, man is not bound by any kind of determinative will except his own. Carnell quotes Corliss Lamont who writes, "Human beings possess true freedom of creative action and are, within reasonable limits, the masters of their own destiny."[46] Humanism does not necessarily rest on theism. Some may choose to link their humanistic values with God but there is no compulsion to do so. "Humanism comes as far as, but refuses to go beyond, the second table of the law."[47] For Carnell, humanism is the point of transition from devotion to impersonal values to the vitalities of personality. As such, it enjoys many advantages. First, the values of humanism are based on persons, not things. Devotion to anything less than living personalities is an affront to the dignity of man.[48] In this sense, the humanist escapes immediacy and its impersonal values. Secondly, humanism stands at the threshold of worthy commitment because of its ability to gladden the heart when devotion to the pursuit of human securities supercedes devotion to immediacy:

> One feels good when he labors for an ideal cause; but he feels better when he labors for real men. Whenever one dares to bring himself to the point where he places his own security in a subordinate position to that of his neighbor, he feels his best. This hierarchy of values in love is quickly recognized by the concerned heart. The instant an individual sacrifices something to make the un- fortunate more secure, that moment there wells up within him a feeling of dignity which can be explained only on the hypothesis that the law of life has been fulfilled. There is an ought written on our heart which commands men to learn the meaning of their own life through fellowship and sacrifice.[49]

To this extent, the humanist stands justified. But this alone is not enough to support one's devotion to humanism as an ultimate value. Carnell was perceptive in exposing the possible fallacies of a devotion to man alone.

First, humanism has tended to serve two masters. It has sought to sustain a delicate balance between devotion to science and devotion to man. Science supplies the method of knowing, and man supplies the values for which we strive.[50] The consequence of this kind of value system is that the humanist, in the role of scientist, has denied the existence of God, any kind of final authority, or any absolute code of moral law. In the role of philosopher, however, the humanist advocates certain a priori ideas (justice, honesty, love, etc.) which he declares that men ought to preserve as human values. The values that he propagates are gained independently of the scientific method which he uses as a basis for the supposition that God is unknowable. Humanism is guilty of using (misusing) science to dismiss the existence of God while the very values that he is preaching were gained a priori. Inconsistency is evident. "Either one must break with science on the finality of human values, and so destroy the ideal of humanism; or he must at least leave open the possibility of God's existence."[51]

Secondly, Carnell argued that humanism promises more than it can deliver. When the humanist altruistically pledges himself to the good of the larger social order (collective ego) he has committed himself to an abstraction, not an individual personality. Further, it is a matter of fact that "a man's uncompromising dedication to the happiness of others may lead to unhappiness on his part."[52] In other words, the humanist encounters a conflict between the collective ego and his individual ego when his personal happiness is at stake. Since it is psychologically impossible to desire one's own unhappiness, the humanist lacks the power (grace) to actualize his intention when the good of others conflicts with the good of self.

Kant called upon man to put aside egotistic motives in favor of a response to law as a rational duty.[53] Appealing to a priori rational arguments, Kant made a good case for his categorical imperative requiring of all men a priori that they should act purely out of a respect for the right. It is the duty of man to be moral. Consciously to desire immorality is to lose self-dignity.

Carnell did not argue against the concept of man's moral duty but he did seriously question the ability of man, unaided by divine grace, to mediate the terms of ethical decision in his own life. And a man is ethical because he acts, not because he knows. Søren Kierkegaard realized as much when he contended that the ethical is nonexistent apart from the act: "The real subject is not the cognitive subject, since in knowing he moves in the sphere of the possible; the real subject is the ethically existing subject."[54] The transcendent self has raised a noble ideal by following the eternal "ought" of an a priori appeal to duty. Moreover, the self loses its dignity if it seeks to run contrary to

the rationes aeternae. But the problem remains because the

self is forced to conclude that there is an uncloseable gap

between what one "ought to be" and "what one actually is."

Reinhold Niebuhr spoke of this predicament:

> The plight of the self is that it cannot do the
> good that it intends. The self in action seems
> impotent to conform its actions to the requirements
> of its essential being, as seen by the self in
> contemplation. The self is so created in freedom that
> it cannot realize itself within itself. It can only
> realize itself in loving relation to its fellows.
> Love is the law of its being. But in practice it
> is always betrayed into self-love. It comprehends
> the world and human relations from itself as the
> centre. It cannot, by willing to do so, strengthen
> the will to do good.[55]

When one attempts to fill the gap between the individual

ego and the collective ego, independent of God, he is doomed

to guilt and condemnation before the self. Either God must

be reintroduced as a means of filling the gap or else man

must be content with the ideal of humanism without the power

to fulfill it, and as such remain unethical. Carnell suc-

cinctly presented what he believed to be the only alternative:

> Humanism has tried to float the second table of
> the law without the dignifying foundation of the
> first, but the experiment has failed. Man has no
> dignity, and thus he is not worthy of our devotion,
> if he does not participate in a transtemporal, trans-
> spatial realm of values which give normative ex-
> pression of the ideal law of life.
> . . . .
> If one balks at the idea of postulating a transcen-
> dental realm of spirit to provide a normative basis
> for law and order in shifting social relations, he
> should be briefed on the implications of his position.
> Since from flux only flux can come, it follows that

it is neither scientific nor rational to define
the categorical imperative as unconditional.
Kant, let us remember, was <u>constrained</u> to rein-
troduce the existence of God into his philosophy.
He knew that without such a postulation the overall unity of rationality would be jeopardized. If
nothing is timelessly obligatory, then it is meaningless to say that it is an obligation that we
treat all men as ends and never as means.

Since we happen to know by nature that the man who
defies the ideal of humanism suffers a disintegra-
tion of his own person, our solution is not a de-
nial of the ideal that humanism stands for. We
must press on beyond humanism to theism, for the
obligations of the one force us to postulate
principles underlying the other.[56]

Carnell has brought us to that point in the value system

where "God" is viewed as the only means of complete satis-

faction to the whole man. But it is an accepted fact that

one can mean many different things when he uses the term

"God." Carnell's insistence is that we come to a proper

(from his perspective, biblical) understanding fo the nature

of God. We can know God only by faith and trust in His

revelation which leads us to a "heart knowledge" of God

through fellowship and communion. God is subject, not

object. Following Augustine, Carnell contends that "we

believe in order that we may know," not vice versa. When we

seek to prove or disprove God, either by discounting Him

or by putting Him into our system, we are going the route

of the philosophers who have never been able to satisfy the

heart. For example, only when we look to the God of the

scriptures do we begin to understand the solution to the

immanence-transcendence controversy:

> One may not personally care to accept the Christian
> view of God and man, but at least he cannot deny
> the axiological advantage of a theology which in
> addition to understanding God as Father, establishes
> both his immanence and his transcendence. . . .
> Transcendence insures the heart that God is far
> enough away from the world to save significance
> for history, while immanence insures it that he
> is near enough to hear prayer and receive worship.
> Whenever this delicate relation is misunderstood,
> the time-eternity balance is upset from one side
> or the other.[57]

Similarly, one can find a solution to the problem of

evil only when he is willing to look to the scriptures and

understand evil in terms of sin:

> This resolution of the problem of evil is not an
> asylum of ignorance. It is the most satisfying
> solution possible because it has been won by a
> battle against the worst form of evil: sin.
> Once the child has learned to love God the Father,
> the abstract rule of good is thrown away. The
> good is what God does. Love will tolerate no
> other condition.[58]

According to Carnell, one will surely despair if one

looks for meaning in history outside of Jesus Christ who

entered time to give a solution to history's contradictions.[59]

Biblical Christianity offers to man a reconciliation with

God on the basis of love and trust. When we, by God's grace,

can love and trust God, we are able to enter into a dimension

of heart satisfying fellowship that the philosopher, deist,

immanentalist, finitist, despairer, or any other thinker

can never enter until he has learned the prerequisite to

fellowship; namely, humility:

Philosophers have never succeeded in satisfying the
heart because the gods they define are able to account for everything but the one thing needful.
The problem of man is the uneasiness of guilt which
gnaws in his heart. Unaware of their own unworthi-
ness even to speak the name of God, therefore,
philosophers tend to deprive themselves of the very
precondition for enjoying fellowship with God.
Love is a gift from God; but God will give it
only to those who declare their complete unworthi-
ness of it. The Lord resists the proud, but he
gives grace to the meek and the humble. Would we
expect a person to act any differently? Pride
always forces love out.

In Jesus Christ the problem of fellowship is solved.
Being love incarnate, he reveals both the love of
God and the conditions which man must meet to receive such love as a gift. There is no thinkable
progression beyond this point. If we leave Christ,
we leave the very law which dignifies our person;
and if we leave the Father of Jesus Christ, we
depart from the only center and source of power
which can transform a life from a hopeless moral
contradiction to tingling pilgrimage of spiritual
promise.[60]

Biblical Christianity

In tracing the weaknesses of various value options Carnel

sought to move from the lower to the higher and finally from

the higher to faith in the person of Christ. Every value

option tested had, to the satisfaction of Carnell, been proven

inadequate to satisfy the complete man. In moving to this

point Carnell attempted to arouse an appetite for Christianity

on the assumption that what he judged to be "Biblical Christi-

anity," with its epistemological and metaphysical framework,

is able to bring axiological happiness to the whole man

(rationally and inwardly). Carnell believed that modern man

had too easily disregarded Christianity. Familiarity breeds

contempt, and modern man has tended more and more to overlook

Christianity, not on the basis of facts, but by prejudgment:

> While each must judge the matter for himself, it
> is the conviction of the Christian philosopher
> that men turn from Biblical Christianity more by
> the leading of prejudgment than by light gained
> from critical hypotheses. It is easy to misunder-
> stand the simple system of Biblical truth by
> confusing it with a dissatisfying denominational
> or institutional system which pretends to come
> in its name. Consequently, men comb the world for
> data with which to deliver them from the uncertain-
> ties of the present hour, while by-passing a copy
> of the Scriptures which may be purchased for a
> few cents in a variety store.[61]

Contrary to those who, in his view, would prejudice the

facts, Carnell contended that Biblical Christianity is the

only axiological commitment which can fully satisfy those

values which men seek by nature.[62] A person with eternal

potentialities can never be finally satisfied with the im-

mediacies of pleasure or materialism. The wisdom of the

philosopher never brings final satisfaction. Humanism left

undignified by a prior devotion to the God of the Scriptures

is an empty commitment; a devotion to man gained a priori

without the power to fulfill the idea. Even a devotion to

God is incapable of satisfying the heart unless the God that

is defined is capable of and interested in entering into

fellowship with man when the proper conditions (humility,

trust, love) are met:

> Christianity places a premium upon the third locus
> of truth--truth in the heart--because man is re-
> lated to God personally; and in all personal affairs
> fellowship rests upon trust. "Without faith (cordial

trust) it is impossible to please him." (Hebrews
11:6) Just as there is no perfection of knowledge beyond acquaintance, so there is no perfection of truth beyond the truthfulness of a good
heart.[63]

Truth in the heart, "that quality of personal character
which coincides with the law of love,"[64] produces fellowship
with God and relates man to the totality of his own person.

Because Christianity deals with man's double environment
it is able to speak satisfactorily to both the head and the
heart, satisfying the whole man. Kierkegaard was correct in
his emphasis on truth as inwardness. Truth as systematic
consistency or propositional correspondence to reality could
never be the basis for fellowship, and without fellowship
man can never attain true happiness. For this reason Carnell,
in his search for an adequate epistemology for axiological
happiness, appealed to a third method of knowing which he
called "knowledge by acquaintance." He was somewhat uneasy
with Kierkegaard's epistemology; Carnell believed that
Kierkegaard had sacrificed too much of the rational element
in truth. While Kierkegaard understood reality from the perspective of the existing, passionate individual, Carnell
contended that Biblical Christianity tempered the concept
of truth in such a way that neither locus could satisfactorily
exist independent of the other. Neither truth as inwardness
nor truth as propositional correspondence to reality enjoys
independent rights. When existentialists insisted on truth
in the heart they were correct because man only finds satisfaction when he relates to God personally. But when

existentialists insisted that "the heart is equipped with

criteria of verification which may be obeyed independently

of, in not in opposition to, the witness of logic,"[65] Carnell

believed them to be wrong. The strength of Christianity lies

in its ability to satisfy the whole man by giving guidance

(by means of the understanding) to the passionate concern of

inwardness:

> God has so tempered truth together that no locus
> may say to another, I have no need of you. Truth
> as reality makes up the environment for fellowship;
> truth as propositional correspondence to reality
> defines the criteria of true fellowship; while
> truth as goodness of character is the fellowship
> itself. These loci must act tunefully if the
> whole man is to be harmoniously related both to
> the universe over against him and to the totality of
> his own person within.

> The faculty of reason has been authorized as the
> responsible guardian of the third locus of truth,
> for apart from its council the heart would never
> fully recognize when the conditions of inward
> truth have been met. For this reason the will
> has no authority to lead the heart into a commitment
> until it has first cleared with the understanding.
> Only the understanding can finally test for error.
> Truth as inwardness may be more important for
> fellowship than truth as a rational system, but
> apart from the guidance which inwardness receives
> from such a system it is a rudderless ship on a
> shoreless sea.[66]

Carnell wholeheartedly believed that Kierkegaard's insis-

tence on a concerned, inward response to God was thoroughly

Christian, but he remained a rationalist to the extent

that "being a rational creature, man must proportion his

spiritual commitments to what the mind can conscientiously

clear."[67] Inwardness is accentuated, not jeopardized, when the mind is satisfied. On this point Carnell and Kierkegaard

were in basic disagreement. Kierkegaard contended that pas-

sionate concern increases in commensurate ratio to objective

uncertainty. An infinite God cannot be deduced from finite

minds. God is wholly other than the world; to base one's

faith on finite knowledge is to slander it.[68] The incarnation

which is nothing less than the absolute paradox, serves as

a perpetual basis for subjective truth--truth that can never

be anything but an offense to reason:

> If the Paradox and the Reason come together in
> a mutual understanding of their unlikeness their
> encounter will be happy, like love's understanding,
> happy in the passion to which we have not yet
> assigned a name, and will postpone naming until
> later. If the encounter is not in understanding
> the relationship becomes unhappy, and this unhappy
> love of the Reason if I may so call it, may be
> characterized more specifically as offense.[69]

Faith takes place when "the self passionately and exi-

stentially believes against the understanding of confronting

the absolute paradox."[70] A leap of inner passion is sine

qua non for genuine Christian faith.[71]

It is at this juncture that we can more specifically

delineate the extent to which Carnell has become existential,

and more specifically, Kierkegaardian, in his Philosophy of

the Christian Religion.

The whole man can never be satisfied with any immediacy.

Only Christian love, experienced through the "heart knowledge"

of fellowship with the person of Jesus Christ, brings ful-

fillment and axiological satisfaction:

And so it turns out that the more we learn about
the meaning of love, the more we learn about the
relation between God and this world. There are
at least two reasons for this. One, God is love
in his eternal essence. Two, when we existentially
realize that we fall short of the duties of love,
we are able to reject self-sufficiency so radically that it becomes natural to rest in God,
morning, noon, and night, every day of the week.
Since the duties of love are directly connected
with eternity, divine grace is relevant to all
stages on life's way.[72]

Love and true existence are the same thing because love

is the law of life. It is the life of love that gives one

authentic existence toward others and personal fellowship

with God.

Carnell was convinced that Kierkegaard had understood

the meaning of Christian love "with a profundity, thoroughness,

and biblical accuracy which, it is no exaggeration to say,

surpassed all previous efforts."[73] Christ placed a premium

on "truth in the heart" because "man is related to God

personally; and in all personal affairs fellowship rests

upon trust."[74]

But while Carnell acknowledged a great indebtedness

to Kierkegaard's insights, the significant differences which

separated them must not be forgotten. Carnell was still as

much a rationalist in A Philosophy of the Christian Religion

as he had been in An Introduction to Christian Apologetics.

He had not sacrificed the intellect when he moved to matters

of the heart; he was simply enlarging the biblical appeal to

the whole man. Knowledge by acquaintance, whereby man is

able to enjoy God's fellowship when the proper conditions

are met, is still an act of rationality:

> The prudent woman does not lavish her affections
> upon the first person she sees approaching. She
> carefully weighs the data, and then, fully per-
> suaded in her mind that it is her lover in the
> distance, releases trust and faith. In like
> manner, one can do justice in his love for God
> only when he first is rationally convinced that
> it is God whom he is fellowshipping with.
>
> When addressing the heart, therefore, the Scriptures
> use rationally intelligible propostions. Spirit
> can be led to the God worthy of being worshipped
> only through the avenue of objectively veracious
> evidences. If our knowledge of God were dis-
> continuous with good scientific-philosophical
> inquiry, we would never know God at all. Faith
> in God is not generically different from faith
> in either another individual or in the body
> of scientifically veracious knowledge. Generic
> faith is a resting of the mind in the sufficiency
> of the evidences. Saving faith may go beyond
> this general expression, but it does not exlude
> it. Whoever does not first have generic faith
> can hardly be said to possess the richer form.
> Even the highest surgings of spiritual ecstasy
> own no powers which are free from the veto
> of the understanding. 'I will pray with the spirit
> and I will pray with the mind also; I will sing
> with the spirit and I will sing with the mind also.
> (I Corinthians 14:15) If Biblical Christianity
> rested on rational paradox or absurdity, it would
> quickly reduce to foolishness.[75]

From what has been said relative to Carnell's extension

of thought it is evident that he was committed to the belief

that "a faith based on rational evidences is able to nourish

a healthy inwardness."[76] Even in time-eternity relations

Carnell believed that there was no convincing reason why the

conventional connections of rational coherence should not

remain. Rationality, for Carnell, was a vital part of the

univocal bond between the two orders of being (God and man)

which increased, not decreased, the passionate concern of

inward faith. Commitment of the whole man to Jesus Christ

is dependent on faith but spirit does not ask us to "leap";

spirit rests in trust when it has been convinced that the

evidences are sufficient. When the self is convinced (mind)

that it is axiologically wise (heart) to commit self to the

person of Jesus Christ, the conditions for fellowship have

been made and the law of love produces authentic existence.

Carnell hoped to achieve his purpose in A Philosophy

of the Christian Religion by broadening Christianity's

appeal and laying a foundation for his next apologetic,

Christian Commitment. The foundation has been laid by taking

away the props on which unbelievers seek to rest:

> Men, who refuse Christ because of presumed 'logical
> errors' in Christianity are men with a self-righteous-
> ness in the area of knowledge. They are resting on
> props which must be pulled away.[77]

Likewise, those who choose values which are incapable of

bringing happiness to the whole man, with respect to the

end as well as the present, are foolish and doomed to ulti-

mate regret. Christianity is not only rationally satisfying,

it is axiologically wise. When men turn from Biblical

Christianity they do so more on the basis of prejudice than

fact:

> If one were to lay his finger on one of the most
> successful prejudices against the Biblical faith,
> it probably is the fear that Christianity is an
> authoritative system of dogma which threatens to
> reduce the total complement of values in a free
> individual. The hedonist fears reduction to a
> negative, Sunday School manner of life; the lover

of bread the choking off of material rights;
the positivist the corrupting of scientific
verification; the philosopher the imposition
of an extra-rational revelation; the humanist
the swallowing up of the dignity of man; the
finitist the loss of goodness; the universalist
the loss of love; the Roman Catholic the loss
of authority; and the existentialist the loss
of creativity.[78]

To be sure, there may be blind spots in the Christian

revelation. The rational man, however, will be satisfied

with that system attended by the fewest difficulties, and

the wise man will choose that value which brings authentic

existence: "Christ did not come to rob us of anything.

He has come to give us life and freedom--and that abundantly."[79]

In the last analysis there is no proof of the pudding apart

from the eating. This became the basis of Carnell's third

and final major apologetic, Christian Commitment.

CHAPTER V

THE MATURE CARNELL

Apologetics is an art. The apologist has no "official"
or universally acceptable method with which he can defend
Christian claims; the defense must be in accordance with
the questions being asked and the current ideas and assumptions which question the trustworthiness of the Christian
faith. So-called defensive apologetics has as its task the
responsibility of replying to specific attacks on the
Christian faith, much as Joseph Butler's The Analogy of
Religion and William Paley's Natural Theology were addressed
to the basic assumptions of their own day. Apologetics of
a more positive nature has as its concern the opening of
dialogue whenever there is a point of contact between religion and culture.

Since traditional conservative theology has tended more
often than not to be on the defensive, it has frequently
failed to see any truth outside the language of Biblical
categories. Often leaping to the conclusion that everything
worth knowing is in the Bible, the conservative tradition
has tended to produce the dreadful effect of separating the
gospel from culture. As a result, the more conservative

113

branches of Christianity often find that they are talking only to themselves. There has been little leadership in showing how the gospel answers questions which the natural man asks about himself and the world. The gospel is thus considered by many to be dated and irrelevant to present concerns.[1]

Carnell envisioned his task as one of being more than a defensive apologist. At best, a defense can only hope to demonstrate that Christian claims are reliable and satisfying to the intellect. However, if the appetite is to be whetted, if the will is to be activated toward Christianity, the apologist must somehow demonstrate both what Christianity has to offer and what it requires. Once apologetics has shown that the claims of Christ are continuous with truth, it is at the end of its task. The rest is left to the proclaiming ministry of the church. Only the Holy Spirit can illuminate the evidences.

Biblical Christianity insists that God is a living person not a metaphysical principle. He must be encountered in the dynamic of personal fellowship. But Carnell insisted that a "rational" and "wise" man will first test the claim of any world view before giving it his total commitment. According to Carnell, but in contrast to more dialectical thinkers, verification enhances the dynamic of personal fellowship with God. At any rate, few theologians have put

their faith more thoroughly to the test of reason and experience than Carnell. He said,

> As long as I have breath, I shall argue that faith
> is a whole-souled response to critically tested
> evidences. To believe in defiance of such evi-
> dences would outrage the image of God in man.[2]

However, Carnell was even more concerned with the positive

chore of showing that the claims of Christ are continuous

with truths to be found in culture. He saw Christianity

in terms of the category which H. Richard Niebuhr called,

"Christ the Transformer of Culture."[3] Carnell belonged to

what Niebuhr classified as the central tradition of Christi-

anity, in that he called for the conversionist answer to the

problem of Christ and culture. He criticized those who de-

sired to make the Church cultic by isolating it from civili-

zation.[4] Carnell's books on apologetics consistently tried

to build on useful points of contact between the gospel and

culture.   In An Introduction to Christian Apologetics the

appeal was to the law of contradiction; in A Philosophy of

the Christian Religion it was to values; in Christian Com-

mitment it was to the judicial sentiment.   In The Kingdom of

Love and the Pride of Life he appealed to the law of love.[5]

Concerning the vital relationship between Christ and culture,

Carnell said:

> If man is made in the image of God (as Scripture
> says he is), then conservatives ought to welcome
> any evidence which helps establish a vital con-
> nection between the healing power of the gospel
> and man as a creature who is plagued by anxiety

and estrangement. A divorce between common and
special grace is an offence to both culture and
the gospel. In our enthusiasm to build on a point
of contact, of course, we may inadvertantly absorb
the gospel into elements of a world system; for
we do not know precisely where common grace leaves
off and special grace begins. But if we are to
get on with our vocation as Christians, we must
accept the risk. Truth is advanced by open dialogue, not by silence.[6]

If Christianity is to be relevant, Carnell felt that

Christians must cease their love affair with abstraction and

begin to speak to concrete and existential needs. The climate

of the modern world is dynamic and existential. While non-

Christians cannot answer the profound question, "How can a

sinner be just before God?", they can discover truths which

help to meet the questions raised by existence itself.

Christians must acknowledge truth wherever it is found. Truth

is not exclusively Christian, but the conservative Biblical

Christian does contend that the revelation of Christ provides

certain answers that are beyond the grasp of the natural man

depending solely on human self-sufficiency.[7] Christianity

does have a profoundly important contribution to make to

human existence. As the later Carnell discovered, however,

this contribution is not in the form of a staid, doleful ac-

ceptance of a world-view. Biblical Christianity is important

in that it reveals an answer to the question of existence

itself, an answer to the question of man's moral predicament

that can only come as one exercises his spiritual as well as

his rational faculties. Authentic existence, which for

Carnell is fellowship with God, comes into being as one meets the demands of his moral and spiritual environment. Christianity is inwardness, and inwardness demands continual ethical decision on the part of the free man. Authentic existence requires more than rational detachment. But, when the free man goes bankrupt in his search for answers to the questions raised by existence, the revelation of Christ's righteousness provides a profound answer. Kierkegaard helped Carnell to understand better the mood of an existential age by asking and answering questions from the perspective of inwardness.

In his later work, Carnell acknowledged an indebtedness to men whose insights he would have rejected in his earlier academic career, when he tended to be more of a defensive apologist, couching his categories in tight Biblical language. In The Kingdom of Love and The Pride of Life Carnell credited Paul Tillich and Sigmund Freud with offering valuable insights into the relevancey of Christian love. And there is basis for arguing that Carnell's method of doing apologetics, especially in his later career, was not far removed from Paul Tillich's way of doing theology; namely, the method of correlation. Carnell's greatest indebtedness, however, was to Søren Kierkegaard. The insights derived from this intellectual friendship constitute the bulk of this chapter.

Inwardness

Kierkegaard, more than any other thinker, led Carnell away from the tendency toward detachment and propositional dependence. Carnell said of his debt to Kierkegaard:

> I must say, it is easy to follow the very one who
> wanted no followers. Without the stimulation of
> the Danish gadfly, I probably would never have
> learned how to ask questions from the perspective
> of inwardness. It is a pleasure to acknowledge my
> indebtedness to Kierkegaard.[8]

The truth which Kierkegaard taught Carnell about in-

wardness was that truth is "a condition of passionate,

ethical inwardness which involves the very being or non-

being of the whole self."[9] Truth, in the ethical sense, is

not simply a given, something that is; truth must "become

as one decides "to be." In his two earlier works, An Intro-

duction to Christian Apologetics and Philosophy of the Christi

Religion, Carnell made room for what he termed propositional

truth and ontological truth,[10] but he had failed to account

for the kind of truth which "comes into being" as one is

transformed by ethical decision in the dialectic of inwardness

This dialectic was especially useful to Kierkegaard in that

it helped him gauge what he called the "stages" on life's way.

Kierkegaard distinguished between three existence-spheres,

called the aesthetic, the ethical, and the religious:

> There are three existence-spheres: the aesthetic,
> the ethical, the religious. The metaphysical is
> abstraction, there is no man who exists metaphysi-
> cally. The metaphysical, ontology, is but it does
> not "exist;" for when it exists it is in the aes-
> thetic, in the ethical, in the religious, and
> when it "is" it is the abstraction of or the "prius"
> for the aesthetic, the ethical, the religious.
> The ethical sphere is only a transitional sphere,
> and hence its highest expression is repentance as

a negative action. The aesthetic sphere is that of immediacy, the ethical that of requirement (and this requirement is so infinite that the individual goes bankrupt), the religious sphere is that of fulfillment, but note, not such a fulfillment as when one fills a cane or a bag with gold, for repentance has made infinite room, and hence the religious contradiction.[11]

To Carnell, Kierkegaard's uniqueness lay in the fact that "no previous thinker," that Carnell had encountered, "had more energetically tried to interpret reality from the perspective of the free, ethical individual."[12] Kierkegaard stressed that love, the law of life, must be understood existentially. To be ethical is to love, and love is more than a rational concept; love manifests itself in "works of love."

However, one must carefully distinguish between Carnell's ethical individual and Kierkegaard's leap from the ethical to the religious sphere of existence. In Christian Commitment Carnell sought to demonstrate that real commitment to God demands moral rectitude. But one must not confuse moral rectitude with legalism. On the contrary, a spiritually honest person will forthrightly acknowledge that the self has failed to close the gap between what it is and what it ought to be. Hopefully, however, the feeling of failure and despair will lead one to a life of faith in Jesus Christ, the gracious provision of God for man's sinfulness. Existentially understood, therefore, the absolute nature of ethics is a means by which the self, confronted with despair, finds its way to a life of faith and hope. Repentance and faith, for

Carnell, have an objective grounding in the person and work of the historical Jesus.

But this approach would not be fully satisfying to Kierkegaard. He would reply that Carnell's theology was still in the ethical, still in the realm of "being," but not yet "becoming." Kierkegaard never predicated his faith in any kind of objectively grounded soteriology. Faith, for Kierkegaard, is a passion, inspired by paradox, which does not permit mediation. One never slides easily from the ethic to the religious by resting in any kind of objective certainty To rest in the universal is to lose oneself as an individual. For the Danish gadfly the individual is higher than the unive

One could talk about truth in terms of values and the law of contradiction (as Carnell did earlier), but the only sense in which one can "be" truth is to meet the demands of his own moral and spiritual existence. What Kierkegaard refer red to as truth which "comes into being" as one is transforme by ethical decision became Carnell's "third rectitude." The ethical gap between what one is and what he ought to be can only be bridged, Carnell contended, when one accepts and meets the moral demands of his own existence. Carnell described the "third kind of truth" in the following manner:

> By the term "third kind of truth" I mean truth as personal rectitude. The possibility of rectitude is implied in the very meaning of moral freedom itself, for uprightness does not come into being until man as he is coincides with man as he ought to be. For example, if one ought to be transformed

by the fact that he is dependent on powers
greater than himself, truth as personal
rectitude has no existence until one morally
and spiritually conforms the whole of his
life to this relation. Essence and existence
are united by right moral decision. If one
chooses to scorn this responsibility, the third
type of truth is shorn of reality.[13]

Like Kierkegaard, Carnell saw man as a synthesis of the
soulish and the bodily.[14] But Carnell's "spirit" is the
crucial part of man's dialectical and creative activity
which makes personal transformation possible by turning
ethical possibility into ethical being. Man's freedom is
his critical distinction from the animal. Freedom gives
man the capacity to make ethical choices. Freedom gives
spirit room to work in its task of opening up to man the
possibility of fulfilling the demands of the imperative essence:[15]

Since man enjoys veto rights over his own impulses, one can only know the content of the
imperative essence by a total spiritual acceptance of the duties to which he is already
committed by existence itself.[16]

Knowledge of the imperative essence can not be known rationally
or empirically; it can only be known by a "moral self-acceptance" of the duties to which one is committed by reason
of his own existence. It is an inward knowledge that must be
answered to existentially. Carnell realized that speculative
philosophy could never give an answer to the moral question:

Man is a spiritual creature; praiseworthy moral
decisions forms the very essence of his dignity.
But if one will not spiritually acquaint himself
with the components of his moral life, nothing
from the outside can move him--whether it be a

system of ethics, a self-transcendent survey of
his own impulses, or a scientific review of how
men conduct themselves in other cultures. The
obligation to meet duty is part of duty. Duty
can never be measured by thought; its essence
eludes detection until one is morally and spiritually controlled by a sense of duty.[17]

One only apprehends the content of the imperative es-

sence when he is spiritually transformed by the duties which

already hold him. In living, we are all confronted with

moral judgments. The image of God in man includes rectitude.

There is an eternal claim on everyone in regards to upright-

ness. In a critical review of Carnell's work, William

Hordern said:

The third way arises from the fact that in living
we have to make moral judgments. Just as the
attempt to deny the logical law of contradiction
finds that it has to use the law, so the denier
of moral knowledge finds himself forced to use it.
But it is a way of knowing that we have to see
within ourselves. External observation of others
will not reveal it adequately.[18]

Whenever one violates the claims of his own sense of

moral duty one violates one's own dignity for human dignity

is the direct result of God's image within man. Whenever

that image is betrayed, whether it be by a violation of the

law of contradiction, false values, a disregard for recti-

tude, or any eternal claim, there is a loss of dignity.

When this loss is the result of our own actions or indif-

ference we have ourselves to blame, but when others fail to

respect the sanctity of our person we are forced to judge

them guilty of violating our dignity. Carnell refers to the

offended moral faculty as the "judicial sentiment":

> We can no more cease judging those who violate
> our rights than we can alter our consecrated
> sense of personal dignity. Unless this point is
> clearly understood, our case will look like
> nothing but an egoistic review of personal dis-
> gruntlement. The problem must be evaluated
> within the moral realities that hold us when
> others outrage our dignity. Whoever refuses to
> meet this condition will never recognize the
> claims of the moral and spiritual environment.
> The third method of knowing must be applied.
> Charging inconsiderate individuals with guilt
> is merely the reverse side of our demand that
> our dignity be respected.[19]

In other words, Carnell is saying that every man is

already committed to a knowledge of God by means of a uni-

vocal bond, a moral absolute, which is based on the as-

sumption that God and man share a common moral and spiritual

environment. However, one cannot enjoy God's fellowship

until one is willing to humbly meet the demands of the im-

perative essence of that environment, which Carnell later

says is love. It is interesting to note that Carnell did

not explain the moral univocality between God and man in

terms of a moral proof of God's existence; his procedure was

simply a purported analysis of morality which reveals that a

knowledge of God is contained within us all, a claim which

Carnell says no honest man can deny.

At this point I must confess that I find the same

problem with Carnell that I find with Kierkegaard. Their

inward, subjective probings nearly always at least imply,

if not explicitly state, that what they find in themselves

is also to be found in others. Perhaps this is the paradoxical advantage and disadvantage of those who have had to
undergo some kind of profound introspection. They find
striking personality patterns in themselves which are all
too often understood as being universally structured. This
is not to say that I deny Carnell's so-called moral and
spiritual environment, but I do question the methodology
whereby Carnell transfers his own experience, introspectively
understood, to others, saying that "no honest man can deny
them."

Carnell believed that his attempt to interpret reality
from the perspective of the free, ethical individual was
in the tradition of Socrates, Pascal, and Kierkegaard who
had attempted to relate the moral sense to the wider problems
of philosophy.[20] Carnell felt that only Kierkegaard, however,
had developed his views into anything resembling a complete
world-view.

Perceptive readers of Kierkegaard and Carnell will
recognize, however, that there are serious differences between them. For example, Kierkegaard sought to solve the
problem of time and eternity without affirming a point of
continuity between God and man. In fact, immanence was the
view of Christianity which Kierkegaard most feared and fought.
He feared that immanence, the view which expresses the conviction "that man is so similar to God, or God is so similar

to man, that a thinking individual can exercise his highest

faculty by merely defining eternal truth in a detached,

objective manner,"[21] would lead to the indifferent attitude

that man is continuous with eternity whether he does anything

about it or not. For Kierkegaard, man must be constantly

shaken out of complacency. Faith "to become" is only pos-

sible when the notion of a peaceful, compatible link between

man and God has been shattered. Paradox, to Kierkegaard,

seemed to be God's way of carrying out this task. Kierkegaard

said:

> If it was paradoxical to posit the eternal truth
> in relationship to an existing individual, it is
> now absolutely paradoxical to posit it in relation-
> ship to such an individual as we have here defined.
> But the more difficult it is made for him to take
> himself out of existence by way of recollection,
> the more profound is the inwardness that his ex-
> istence may have in existence; and when it is made
> impossible for him, when he is held so fast in
> existence that the backdoor of recollection is
> forever closed to him, then his inwardness will
> be the most profound possible. . . .There can be
> no stronger expression for inwardness than when
> the retreat out of existence into the eternal by
> way of recollection is impossible; and when, with
> truth confronting the individual as a paradox,
> gripped in the anguish and pain of sin, facing
> the tremendous risk of the objective insecurity,
> the individual believes.[22]

Thus, Carnell sees Kierkegaard's delight with paradox

as an extension of his rejection of immanence.[23] Immanence

must be shattered by transcendence and objective thinking

by paradox. Kierkegaard's rejection of immanence is pre-

cisely his objection to the ethical. The answer to complacency,

for Kierkegaard, is a leap of faith in the face of uncertainty, an abandonment of the ethical for the religious.

There are similarities and differences between Carnell's view of immanence and the kind of indolent immanence to which Kierkegaard addressed his scorn. From an introspective point of view, Carnell contended:

> If modern theologians would only heed the realities that already hold them, they would immediately perceive that most of the debate about "point of contact" is mere sophomoric quibbling. God is "wholly other" only in a very special sense. One cannot even walk down the street without participating in a moral and spiritual environment that is common to both God and an upright man. God is immanent as well as transcendent. Theologians ought to recognize that when others are unkind to them, or when their rights are violated, the judicial sentiment is aroused; and that the judicial sentiment, on analysis, is the voice of a moral tribunal that outreaches human authority.[24]

There can be no doubt that Carnell's later work was too "ethical" for Kierkegaard. But for that matter, his work throughout had been one of emphasis on contact between the gospel and culture by reason of the image of God in man. Carnell concluded:

> Since man is made in the image of God, man shares in the life of God whenever he makes contact with ultimate elements in either the rational, aesthetic, or moral and spiritual environment. The true, the beautiful, and the good find their metaphysical status in God. And man comprehends each sphere through a specific point of contact; the law of contradiction, the law of proportion, and the law of life respectively. God is truth; God is beauty; and God is love.[25]

In <u>Christian Commitment</u> Carnell limited his inquiry to the third method of knowing where contact between time and

eternity is made possible because of the moral and spiritual
environment which holds God perfectly and an upright man
imperfectly. Carnell says:

> I now mean, even as I shall continue to mean, that
> the moral and spiritual environment on the finite
> level and spiritual environment on the divine level;
> and that it is not improper to say that God is
> perfectly held by standards that hold an upright
> man imperfectly.[26]

This is not meant to imply pantheism. Carnell makes
it clear that he is speaking of a common environment and not
a common essence.[27] Such common ground makes it possible
to make meaningful predications about God. Furthermore, it
makes the veracity of God given through revelation meaningful
in that "all truth in a Revelation presupposes a conviction
that God's attributes are the same, in all but degree, with
the best human attributes."[28] It should be noted that this
view carries its own implications about the freedom of God.
God is only free to act in accordance with his nature.
Carnell says, "God completes the moral cycle out of a necessity that resides in his own character."[29]

   We must now closely examine what Carnell has said about
the univocal point of identity between time and eternity.
On the one hand, Carnell affirmed, rather than denied, the
possibility of knowledge and certainty about the possibility
of knowledge and certainty about the truth of God. Kierkegaard
did not ally objective certainty and passion, but Carnell
claimed to the end that "passion and certainty are friends,

128

not foes."[30] Carnell did not believe that Biblical Christi-

anity asks the heart to accept what the head rejects, but

Kierkegaard insisted that it must if selfhood were to be

gained. On the other hand, Carnell had an increasing awarene

of the limitations of reason and of an "objective" knowledge

of God. In A Philosophy of the Christian Religion Carnell

carefully demonstrated that "knowledge by acquaintance" is

of greater value than knowledge by inference. One cannot

experience fellowship through objective knowledge; knowledge

by acquaintance is made possible only through moral rectitude

Since fellowship with God is dependent on uprightness, moral

truth and authentic existence only come into being as one

meets the demands of the imperative essence through ethical

decision. Carnell stated:

> If we submit to a particular book, church, or
> priestly caste, does it mean that we no longer
> need to make decisions that decide our destiny?
> If so, the counsel of Kierkegaard is again ger-
> mane. Whenever individuals rely on objective
> security as an escape from moral decision, they
> jeopardize their own individuality. It would
> hardly be appropriate to repeat Kierkegaard's
> incisive arguments here. We need only say,
> as he has said before, that individuality con-
> sists in ethical decision; for the real man is
> the moral man. Neither book, church, nor priest-
> ly caste can relieve us of the responsibility of
> closing the gap between the descriptive essence
> and the imperative essence; and any attempt to
> do so would rob us of selfhood.[31]

Some have suggested that Carnell's later work represents

a trend within theological conservatism which threatens to

"replay the errors of earlier modernism by returning to

an overconfidence in man's goodness and rationality due to an uncritical and unsound view of the immanence of God."[32] However, I believe this view is unwarranted and perhaps precipitated by too hasty a reading of Carnell. It is true that Carnell moved away from the conservative theological position which denied any point of contact between culture and the gospel,[33] but he never indicated that he believed that fellowship with God could become a reality until God graciously takes the initiative and enters time. The gospel, for Carnell, is, as it has always been, a gospel of grace. He believed with Kierkegaard that "the incarnation is an indictment of that conceit in human nature which imagines that man can close the gap between time and eternity by rationally moving upward."[34] The paradox of morals is that moral rectitude cannot be aroused by rational or volitional striving. An upright heart is a gift of God, given when one freely chooses to submit his affections to the transforming power of the moral and spiritual environment.[35]

Kant's approach to God seems on the surface to be similar to Carnell's epistemology of moral self-acceptance. But closer inspection reveals that Carnell's moral and spiritual environment is more than one's conscience rendering an a priori verdict against the soul. Carnell's contention is that the "conscience is the subjective principle of responsibility for one's deeds before the divine tribunal."[36] But

the judicial sentiment, the judgments we make upon those
who fail to respect the dignity of our person, is God's
moral absolute, not subject to social and cultural conditioning."[37] Carnell, says:

> Since we are held by a sense of our own spiritual
> dignity from existence itself, it follows that the
> roots of our moral life go deeper than cultural
> conditioning. The intuition of our dignity is
> drawn from the moral and spiritual environment;
> it is not an acquired characteristic. An aroused
> judicial sentiment is merely heaven's warning
> that the image of God is being outraged. Cultural
> conditioning may alter the direction of the
> judicial sentiment, but it does not alter the
> faculty itself. Our participation in God issues
> in a spiritual intuition of our own dignity,
> on the one hand, and the guilt of those who vio-
> late it, on the other.[38]

It is not difficult to agree with Carnell's protest
against the kind of Darwinian relativism which causes some
to speak of man merely following dominant instincts, doing
the stuff of an animal. It seems more reasonable and
realistic to give credence to the view that man's moral life
goes much deeper than biological and cultural conditioning.
On the other hand, Carnell perhaps goes too far when he
too closely identifies men's judgments of others with the
judgment of God. Since Carnell has already admitted that
ethics depends upon self-love, it would appear that our
judgments of others could be and are clouded by self-interest
Further, Carnell seems to be violating one of his earlier
axiomatic principles; namely, that the affects of sin on the
Imago Dei leave one's judgments impaired and unreliable.

Just as Carnell himself cautions about depending on conscience
to lead one to God because of its chameleonic tendencies,
it would seem that one would have to avoid using one's own
judgments as a criterion of rectitude, because of inherent
self-righteous tendencies.

In regard to Kant, Carnell believed that Kant's approach
to morals had proved inadequate. Kant was right, Carnell
says, in his "insistence that there is no good but a good
will, but he was materially wrong when he defined the good
will as a purely rational regard for laws of self-consistent
conduct."[39] Kant was unable to see that fellowship is
superior to thought and that the vital, loving, man is
spiritually superior to the rational man. It was Kierkegaard
who took love, placed an existential interpretation on it,
and guided Carnell to the understanding that love and true
existence are the same thing, for love is the law of life.

Love Is Truth

Thus far we have attempted to demonstrate Carnell's
debt to Kierkegaard for his insistence that the real man is
the moral man and that the moral man only comes into being
as he mediates eternity in time through passionate, ethical
decision. This kind of truth (truth as rectitude) only
comes into being when God closes the gap between what one is
and what one ought to be. What one ought to be is what
Carnell has called throughout the "imperative essence." But

now it is time to ask, what is the guiding criterion by

which one can define a truly upright life? Again, Kierkegaard

insights were for Carnell as a guiding star:

> He (Kierkegaard) was convinced--and rightly so--
> that far too many ethicists were quagmired in
> legalism. Consequently, the prevailing moral
> standards in Christianity seemed to be more rele-
> vant to the Old Testament than to the New.[40]

Kierkegaard recognized that "love is the fulfillment of law,

and that the ethical self falls short of its duties until it

performs works of love."[41] Love is the pith and marrow of

the imperative essence. Without "works of love" the indi-

vidual never has true existence, for love is the law of life.

In essence, Carnell concluded that Kierkegaard's thesis,

"Truth is subjectivity," meant the same thing as saying

for Christianity that "Truth is love." Love is a point

of union between the temporal and the eternal, subsistence

and true existence. Love is the most important condition

of inwardness. Carnell said of Kierkegaard's regard for love:

> Love cannot be stored up, like insect specimens
> or jars of water. Love is vitally related to
> the individual, for the individual remains only
> a spiritual potentiality until his capacity for
> love is released. This means that the thesis,
> "Truth is subjectivity," is but another way of
> stating the Christian conviction that truth is
> love, and that the ethical manners of the living
> person give reality to the substance of love.
> Therefore, whenever a person turns from the task
> of love, he actually turns from himself. He gives
> up individual existence--spiritually and existen-
> tially understood. He may continue to occupy
> space, to be sure; but this is nothing of which
> to boast, for corpses also continue to occupy
> space.[42]

After carefully examining the merits of "justice" and "consideration" as possible fulfillments of the imperative essence Carnell concluded that the mystery of selfhood lies beyond all rational and legal hope which they represent. "Justice and consideration only answer to as much of our person as we happen to reveal."[43] Justice, which is based on one's similarity to his race, and consideration, which is based on one's difference to the race, are fruits of rectitude, but they could never be the law of life.

Carnell's high regard for Reinhold Niebuhr as a moralist was due in part to Niebuhr's brilliant treatment of love and justice.[44] Both Carnell and Niebuhr realized that the ethic which controls the individual cannot inform the group. From the perspective of society the highest moral ideal is justice. The need for justice arises out or the need to restrict the self-interest of others from encroaching upon the rights and privileges of a neighbor. Consideration surpasses the law of justice, at least for Carnell, in that a considerate individual can go beyond the law. A considerate person realizes that personality is unique; it baffles all rational expectations. Therefore, one must be willing to consider others despite differences and deviations. But love, the law of life, for the individual "is oriented by only one vertical religious reference, to the will of God; and the will of God is defined in terms of all-inclusive love."[45]

Love is greater in that it never asks for uniformity,

only love. God looks only for love. Even doctrinal

orthodoxy is nothing if a man has not love.[46] As Carnell

said, "Love comprises the stuff of rectitude, the third

type of truth, the imperative essence, the law of life, the

moral and spiritual environment, and the essence of God."[47]

But little, if anything, can be said about a formal defini-

tion of love.

> Since love has no existence apart from an act
> of love, it is impossible to give a rationally
> accurate account of its essence. It can be known
> only as one loves or is loved. Knowledge by
> inference must yield to knowledge by acquaintance.[48]

Thy Kingdom Come . . . .

Upon establishing the fact that love is the stuff of

rectitude and the imperative essence, Carnell presented the

moral predicament:

> If God judges us by the heights of the law of love,
> we are in a perilous moral position, for we simply
> do not have natural affections for the careless
> multitudes who crowd the highways, who compete with
> us for cafeteria tables, and who scatter beer cans
> and watermelon rinds around our favorite picnic
> areas. Merely getting along with others, let alone
> loving them, is a very taxing responsibility.[49]

That which Kant says we ought to do, Christianity says

we are unable to do. Love cannot be properly motivated by

rational or legal necessity; it must come as the fruit of

affections which have been transformed by God. The paradox

of the moral predicament is that, on the one hand, "love

is a fruit, not a work; it is unconscious of any lawful sense

of obligation."[50] On the other hand, "not only are we

obliged by the law of love, but in a very meaningful sense

we are natively capable of meeting it."[51] With this in mind,

Carnell argues that the logic of repentence is very compelling.

He says:

> Were we to postpone repentance, therefore, we
> would simply prove that our affections are dom-
> inated by pride, rather than humility. A refusal
> to repent betrays one of two things: either one
> disbelieves that his life is morally ambiguous,
> and thus nurses the false expectation that he
> conforms to rectitude; or he senses his distance
> from rectitude, but clings to the undefined hope
> that some legally satisfying way out can be found.
> In either case he flies in the face of truth.
> He may be able to plot the course of single stones,
> but when he confronts the landslide of a totally
> self-centered life, no escape by rational calcu-
> lation is possible. Emergency action is the order
> of the day; and this action, as proved by the third
> method of knowing, is repentance.[52]

Since man is held responsible for laws which evil af-

fections keep him from keeping, God has provided "indirect

fulfillment" as well as "direct fulfillment" of our moral

experience. Repentance is simply a spontaneously expressed

sorrow for having failed. Carnell judged Kant guilty of not

seeing the logic of repentance. He said of Kant:

> Kant restricted himself to what I call "direct
> fulfillment." A law cannot bind us unless we
> have resident moral ability to fulfill it.
> Such an approach is unacceptable, however, for
> it contradicts one of the most patent parts of
> our moral experience--that of "indirect ful-
> fillment." Judged from within moral self-
> acceptance, an individual can satisfy rectitude
> in two different ways: either by spontaneously
> doing what is right or by spontaneously expres-
> sing sorrow for having failed. The gentle life
> is direct fulfillment, while the penitent life
> is indirect fulfillment. Both satisfy the claims
> of the moral and spiritual environment. Kant
> made the Pelagian mistake of thinking that man
> can only be held responsible for laws that he
> can directly meet.[53]

Realizing one's own limitations and inability to meet
the imperative duties is the first step toward "indirect
fulfillment." As a source of truth, reason has reached the
end of its tether. Reason declares man guilty and demands
punishment, but reason and philosophy have their limitations.
As the Scriptures attest, "man by wisdom knows not God."
The appeal is to forsake the pride of life and seek the
kingdom of love. The kingdom of God is a kingdom of love.
Christ is the wisdom and power of that kingdom; He "pro-
pitiated the judicial sentiment in God by his active and
passive obedience."[54] When men repent, accepting God's
provision of love, they enter into a fellowship, a kingdom,
that is forever contingent on one law--the law of love. The
moral man is a loving man. Fellowship with God is not possible through intellectual detachment; it is the experience
of being loved. An intellectual account of love can never
provide the substance of a happy life.

Children are among the first to recognize love as a
medium of knowledge. In his book, The Kingdom of Love and
the Pride of Life, Carnell had much to say about the intuitive insights of happy children. He said:

> Since happy children are citizens of the kingdom
> of love, they enjoy an intuitive perception of
> virtue. When adults are asked to tell what virtue
> is, they often give the impression that the task
> is beyond their capacity. Haven't the greatest
> philosophers failed to agree on a definition?
> How, then, can common people succeed? If happy
> children were to hear of this, they might be some-
> what amused, for they discover the meaning of virtue

by listening to their own hearts. Whether the
intellect will own it or not, the heart has its
convictions. These convictions say that a person
is good when he is kind and truthful, and that in
the end a good person has nothing to fear. The
first part clarifies love, while the second part
clarifies hope. To love is to be kind and truthful, to hope is to believe that things will work
out happily in the end. The issue is as simple
as that.[55]

Kierkegaard, I believe, would concur with Carnell in saying

that truth is love. To turn from love is to turn from one-

self and the kingdom. Kierkegaard said:

To defraud oneself of love is the most terrible
deception of all. It is an eternal loss for which
there is no compensation either here or in eternity.[56]

Being the only complete individual, Jesus Christ met

the absolute terms of the law of love at every moment in

his life. He was truth. Kierkegaard described it this way:

Christ became the destruction of the law, because
He was what it demanded, its destruction, its end;
for when the demand is fulfilled, the demand exists
only in the fulfillment, but hence it no longer
exists anywhere as demand. . . .Moreover, He was love,
and His love was the fulness of the law. "No
one could convict Him of any sin," not even the law
which knows every conscience; "there was no deceit
in his mouth," but everything in him was truth;
there was in his love not the hairs-breadth of a
moment, of an emotion, of an interval between his
purpose and the demand of the law for its fulfillment.
He did not say "no," like that one brother or "yes"
like the other brother, for His meat was to do His
Father's will; thus He was one with the Father, one
with every demand of the law, so its perfecting was
a necessity to Him, His sole need in life. The love
in Him was perpetually active; there was no moment,
not one single instant in His whole life when His
love was merely a passive feeling which seeks
expression while it lets time pass; or a mood
which produces a self-satisfaction and dwells on
itself while the task is neglected. No, His love
was expressed in perpetual activity; even when He
wept, was this not redeeming the time?[57]

An existential interpretation of love demands suffering, but both Kierkegaard and Carnell concluded that
true Christianity requires it. Whenever a Christian honors
the conditions of inwardness; faith, suffering, hope, and
love, he can be sure that he is doing all that is required
of him.[58] The conditions of inwardness insure a continual
dynamism in the lives of those who choose to call themselves
Christian.

> Whenever a person turns from the infinite duty
> of love, he turns from Christianity itself.
> A Christian, if he is serious about his religious
> devotion, will tack passionately between infinite
> duty and the pain of temporal failure. In short,
> he will express repentance as well as love. Re-
> pentance is a mark of humility; it is nourished
> through faith and hope and the general experience
> of suffering.[59]

Those who refuse to heed the word of the gospel again
demonstrate that man's problem is not a lack of knowledge,
but a lack of moral courage to act on the knowledge he
already has.[60] "What standard could one meet that Christ
has not already met?"[61] Having defended the truthfulness of
the Christian claim, Carnell was content in recognizing the
limitations of apologetics.

> Once apologetics has shown that the claims of
> Christ are continuous with truth, it is at the
> end of its tether. It cannot, even as it would
> not want to, encroach on the preaching ministry
> of the church. God is a living person, not a
> metaphysical principle. Evidences may point to
> God, but God himself must be encountered in the
> dynamic of personal fellowship. Only the Holy
> Spirit can illuminate the evidences.[62]

The invitation to fellowship is God's. "Behold I stand at the door and knock; if any one hears my voice and opens the door, I will come in to him and eat with him, and he with me" (Revelation 3:20). But every man must open the door from the inside.

Chapter VI

EDWARD JOHN CARNELL: AN EVALUATION

The Quest For A Balanced Apologetical Method

In his major writings Edward John Carnell put his
conservatively interpreted view of Christianity to the test
in three major domains: reason, value theory, and human
existence.   Carnell found Christianity to be satisfying in
every area.

The entirety of Carnell's first apologetic, An Introduction to Christian Apologetics (1948), was devoted to a
closely reasoned argument for conservative biblical Christianity.   Carnell's appeal was to the rational man.   He argued
that Christianity is more reasonable and better able to
explain the facts of existence coherently than any alternative world view.   As a leading spokesman for the new conservatism, Carnell attempted to close the mouths of those
who criticized the conservative interpretation of Christianity
with being irrational.[1]   But he opened the door for new
criticism from those within the newly risen post World War
I phenomenon of neo-orthodoxy.   The new theology not only
rejected the immanence of the liberals -- it also rejected
the conservative's view of propositional revelation as yet
another form of continuity.   The so-called "crisis" theologian
spoke of revelation as something which man experiences in the
encounter with God, the existential commitment.

Carnell recognized that the new climate of opinion gen-
erated by the new theology was more subjective, non-rational,
and existential in tenor and approach. But this did not
stalemate his apologetic; Carnell believed that Christianity
could account for the subjective as well as the rational
aspect of man. He made this transition in A Philosophy of
the Christian Religion (1952) by demonstrating that Christianity is more than a metaphysical principle; Christianity
is the wisest value modern man can choose because it goes
beyond the immediacies of life and knowledge by inference
to the more personal and heart satisfying value of fellowship
with God by means of a "knowledge by acquaintance."

Heavily influenced by Kierkegaard's method of asking
questions from the standpoint of inwardness, Carnell placed
an even greater emphasis on the existential and introspective
approach in his two later apologetical works, Christian
Commitment and The Kingdom of Love and the Pride of Life.
The strength of this later work, in addition to broadening
his apologetical perspective, was Carnell's emphasis upon
the meaning of true Christian commitment. The obstacle to
commitment is not, he stressed, so much a lack of knowledge
as it is the failure to act on the knowledge one already has.
To enjoy God's fellowship is infinitely more important than
simply knowing about God.

In these areas Carnell seemed to believe that he had
done all that he could. The rest he was content to leave to

the preaching ministry of the church and the illuminating
of the evidence by the Holy Spirit.

Christian Apologetics is Christianity defensively
stated. There are as many opinions as to what constitutes
an adequate apologetic as there are interpretations of
Christianity itself. An apologetic is always judged from
some point of view, just as it is done from some point of
view. Consequently, one could critique Carnell from the
perspective of any religious philosophy. A devotee of
Kierkegaard would undoubtedly criticize Carnell's attempt
to test the truths of revelation against the facts of history,
science, and the canons of reason. While a strict empiricist would deny the use Carnell made of a priori knowledge
and Carnell's whole concept of "systematic consistency."
The biblical dogmatist, on the other hand, would insist
that neither the inductivist nor the a priori reasoner can
test the ultimate truth of revelation by any fact or principle
apart from the revelation itself.

Because Carnell combined various philosophical methods,
he opened his religious philosophy to criticism from practically all dogmatic types. But rather than commit himself
to an exclusive methodology, he chose to work with the truths
which he could draw from various philosophical traditions.
From the rationalist he learned the essential significance
of consistency; from the empiricist the importance of coherence
from the existentialist the meaning of inwardness. And from
his own conservative Christian upbringing Carnell learned

to relate all of these truths to the one absolute criterion of truth -- the mind of God as revealed in Scripture. By broadening his apologetic method Carnell gave his apologetic the widest possible appeal.

Carnell was not a detached theologian speaking from the standpoint of a thinker interested only in intellectual games or theological narcissism. He was seriously interested in the problems of the Church, and the preaching and teaching ministries with which the Church is charged were always in his mind. The concern of the Church, Carnell contended, is truth -- especially the truth as revealed in Jesus Christ. However, when the Church finds truth in culture that is continuous with the claims of Christ, it should be welcomed.

As a Christian apologist, Carnell sought to establish contact with culture on several levels. In his later work his primary concern was to relate certain existential elements in Christianity to the rich dialectical existentialism of Kierkegaard. To a certain extent, this endeavor was successful. And even though many of Carnell's readers know less about Christian Commitment than they do of his other works, Carnell considered this to be his best book. Interestingly enough, however, this book best illustrates the limitations of Carnell's somewhat eclectic approach to apologetics.[2] Like Kierkegaard, Carnell was convincing in his assertion that Christianity is continually demanding of the will a total commitment. But Carnell was fated to end up on a deadend street by following Kierkegaard too closely. Carnell was never as dialectical as Kierkegaard. While

Kierkegaard insisted that one must make a "leap" from the
ethical to the religious sphere of existence, Carnell believed
that one should know before he leaps. Subjective faith could
not supplant reason as a necessary basis for Christian commitment for Carnell. He retained the conservative emphasis
upon faith as trust in the divine revelation given through
the Bible -- a trust warranted by the Bible's moral appeal
and its miraculous evidences. But what we are called upon to
believe and trust in, Carnell asserted, does not violate the
criteria established by right reason. Carnell's respect for
the faculty of reason, even in matters concerning the eternal,
placed necessary limitations on his existential perspective.
His emphasis upon inwardness was also limited by his understanding of the propositional language of Scripture, which
Carnell considered normative. He did not believe the
language was always capable of expressing reality, but he
did believe that there is a real relation between the reason
that language represents and the reason to be found in man
as a part of the Imago Dei. Thus, Carnell's mature interpretation of Christianity, though much influenced and informed by
Kierkegaardian existentialism, never included the radical
contention that Christian commitment demands a totally
non-rational "leap of faith."

The strength of Carnell's method, from the conservative
perspective, lay in the fact that it allowed Carnell to
avoid the extremes of existentialist theology. Thus, he

was able to produce an apologetic that put Biblical

Christianity into an existential perspective acceptable

to the normative standards of conservative Christianity.

The Quest for a Balanced View of Revelation

Carnell's views on revelation were formulated against

the backdrop of theological liberalism and neo-orthodoxy,

and he reacted strongly against what he believed to be a

depreciation of normative elements in revelation by spokesmen

for these movements. He believed that many liberals had de-

preciated normative elements out of a zeal for humanistic

creativity; neo-orthodoxy, out of a zeal for revelation as a

disclosure of the Divine person. In a revealing statement

of his quest for a balanced view of revelation, Carnell wrote:

> Protestants must recover the Reformation balance
> between revelation as a disclosure of God's <u>person</u>
> and revelation as a disclosure of God's <u>will.</u> The
> first is mystical and inward; the second, objective
> and propositional. If we drive a wedge between
> personal and propositional revelation, we evacuate
> Christian theology of its normative elements. In
> this event, our conversation about faith reduces to
> an exercise in aesthetics. . . .
>
> Let me give the pith and marrow of what I am trying
> to say. If Protestants fail to distinguish between
> apostolic testimony and their own interpretation
> of this testimony, they corrupt the Protestant
> principle by slighting the threshold of variable
> error that attends all biblical exegesis. They
> return to the ethos of Roman Catholicism. But if
> Protestants make this distinction and yet refuse
> to improve their interpretation by submitting to
> apostolic testimony, they corrupt the Protestant
> principle by making themselves equal with the
> apostles. They repudiate the normative elements in
> Christian theology. The first error overlooks the
> work of sin in theological inquiry; the second, the
> authority of _____

the apostles in detecting and correcting this
work. If orthodoxy tends to make the first
error, liberalism and neo-orthodoxy tend to make
the second.[3]

Theologians outside of conservative ranks were often

critical of Carnell's view of revelation. From the liberal

perspective, Harold DeWolf maintained that Carnell was

"formally committed more closely to sole dependence on

the words of the Bible. . . than the rest of his thought

can justify."[4] Oddly enough, this view was shared by

many hardcore conservatives who saw Carnell as a wavering

and even wayward evangelical. DeWolf also considered

Carnell's doctrine of the atonement legalistic and his view

of divine justice as retaliating, irrational, and sub-

Christian.[5]

Speaking from the standpoint of neo-orthodoxy, William

Hordern saw Carnell's view of plenary inspiration and propo-

sitional revelation as being unjustifiable. Hordern spoke

of this doctrine as "a doctrine that embarrasses without

helping the Christian cause."[6]

Yet, on the whole, Hordern was complimentary toward

Carnell's work. Carnell was likened to a breath of fresh

air which promised to blow away the staleness of the funda-

mentalist-modernist impasse. Just as theologians of various

schools had been repenting for the sins of modernism, men

like Carl Henry and John Carnell were finally repenting for

the sins of fundamentalism.[7]

Much of Carnell's contribution lay in the fact that his theology provided a balanced view of the subjective and objective aspects of revelation. Carnell acknowledged that one cannot know God as a person through an external medium, yet he believed that it is necessary to preserve the traditional belief in a propositional conveyance of truth such as we have in the Protestant canon of the Bible. He was suspicious of the subjectivism and skepticism which he believed attends every religious epistemology which is not grounded in the objective authority of Christ's person and will as witnessed by the apostolate. Yet he stressed the superiority of "knowledge by acquaintance" over "knowledge by inference." Carnell encouraged many non-conservative theologians to believe that the time for fresh meaningful dialogue on the meaning of revelation was approaching. Representatives of both the liberal and the neo-orthodox tradition have agreed that Carnell did more than any conservative theologian of recent times to open the door for creative discussion among differing viewpoints.[8]

Carnell the Prophet

Even though he had been nurtured by conservatives, Carnell did not always feel completely at home in his own theological tradition. Carnell called himself "orthodox" because he assented to the great doctrines of the faith. But he refused to identify with those attitudes which he considered "cultic"

remnants of his fundamentalist heritage. It is no secret
that Carnell suffered from incessant insomnia and from
nervous disorders during long periods of his relatively short
life. And it is the opinion of some of those who know him
best that his internal conflicts were largely caused by the
fact that he was in one way a conservative; in another way
he was a person in process with the willingness to change in
the interest of truth.

The kind of emotional and intellectual autonomy which
Carnell struggled for has been characterized by Karl Menninger
the well-known American psychiatrist, in an analogy he once
made between a hooked fish and a human being entrapped by
his intellectual and social environment. Menninger observed:

> When a trout rising to a fly gets hooked on a
> line and finds himself unable to swim about
> freely, he begins with a fight which results
> in struggles and splashes and sometimes an
> escape. Often, of course, the situation is
> too tough for him.
>
> In the same way the human being struggles with
> his environment and with the hooks that catch
> him. Sometimes he masters his difficulties;
> sometimes they are too much for him. His strug-
> gles are all that the world sees and it naturally
> misunderstands them. It is hard for a free fish
> to understand what is happening to a hooked one.[9]

While Carnell's ontological and epistemological starting
points may be more important than his psychological starting
point for understanding his theology, Carnell, the critic,
cannot be understood apart from the conflicts within him
which gave rise to a prophetic element in his writings and in
his teaching.

The crowning error of most fundamentalists, Carnell believed, is that they tend to equate the possession of revealed truth with the possession of virtue -- the result of which is legalism, a quest for status by negation, and separatism. Carnell believed that this error stemmed from a lack of clarification on the distinction between the biblical doctrines of justification and sanctification, and he asserted that it was a serious error in that it generally produces a "cultic" attitude in Christian believers. For this reason, he preferred to think of himself as a religious conservative, interested in restoring the classical lines of orthodoxy, not as a fundamentalist.

In his book, <u>The Case for Orthodox Theology</u> (1960) Carnell raised questions about the unity of the Church which created confusion not only about his own point of view but also about the position of conservatism in general. Gresham Machen, one of the earlier and most capable spokesmen for fundamentalists, had implied that there is a need for separation in the church when the essence of Christianity is at stake. In Machen's words:

> We are not dealing with delicate personal questions: we are not presuming to say whether such and such an individual man is a Christian or not. God only can decide such questions; no man can say with assurance whether the attitude of certain individual "liberals" toward Christ is saving faith or not. But one thing is perfectly plain -- whether or not liberals are Christians, it is at any rate perfectly clear that liberalism is not Christianity. And that being the case, it is highly undesirable that liberalism and Christianity should continue to be propagated within the bounds of the same organization.[10]

Carnell rejected Machen's views on separatism, regarding
any view which denies the "fellowship of all who share in the
blessings of the Abrahamic covenant" as separatist in nature,
thus "cultic." Many fundamentalists alienated themselves
from Carnell after his views toward Machen became known. And
he received biting criticism from many who had formerly considered him as their own spokesman. His remarks were dubbed
deficient, pseudo-ecumenical, and non-representative of the
evangelical position.[11]

Indeed, Carnell's willingness to stand detached enough
from his own tradition to be critical of its self-righteous
tendencies is to be commended. But it does seem that Carnell
somewhat over-simplified the concept of separatism. He seems
to have raised more questions than he answered concerning
the doctrine of the church. Carnell's usual careful articulation of an intellectual position was not as evident in
his discussions of "separatism" and the "cultic" as it was
in other areas. But the motive behind the concern was
commendable. Carnell was seeking to combat the fundamentalist tendency to equate the possession of truth with the
possession of virtue. Such non sequitur reasoning often
led many to conclude that since only fundamentalists were
in possession of truth, they alone were virtuous enough to
form the body of Christ. All other elements in the Christian
community were apostate.

On such grounds, fundamentalists had driven a self-
righteous wedge between themselves and the church universal.

Carnell sought to help remove the wedge by pointing out the intellectual and moral errors in his own tradition which had blocked communication. For that concern the Church is indebted to Edward John Carnell.

An Apologist to the Tough-Minded

Carnell's defense of a coherent biblical text, consistent with the facts of history and science, was not, of course, without its serious difficulties. If he is consistent and if he takes the apologetic task seriously, the apologist who holds this view of revelation is continually forced into the position of defending the faith against every historical and scientific fact which purportedly threatens the coherence of the revelation. But Carnell was such an apologist. He stood his ground on every issue that he believed warranted an answer, and he built his case for orthodox Christianity on the basis of what he considered sufficient evidence. Carnell's forte was philosophical apologetics, but in An Introduction to Christian Apologetics Carnell spent at least half of the book defending Christian truth claims against specific problems. In A Philosophy of the Christian Religion the entire book was given to a defense of the Christian value option. Carnell's supposition regarding the nature of Christian truth dictated the polemical tenor of his early writings.

Carnell emphasized that a distinction exists between personal and impersonal knowledge. He knew that science and philosophy have no access to the essence of personality, that "in the instance of personality, knowledge by inference must yield to knowledge by acquaintance,"[12] but he never accepted the validity of a faith not grounded in reason. Carnell consistently maintained that encounter involves a blending of "intellectual assent and spiritual commitment without any consciousness that one is leaving one realm of evidences for another."[13] He considered the "thou-truth" and "it-truth" distinction an ad hoc hypothesis of theologians

> Evangelical encounter is man's whole-souled response to rationally objective evidences. Unless the whole man can be brought into the act of worship, one does not wholly worship. He must hold back some part, usually his intellect. But God never asks a man to bifurcate himself. Man does not encounter "thou-truth" on Sunday and "it-truth" the rest of the week. Any contact with truth is tantamount to contact with God, for God is truth. God illuminates the mind to perceive truth, and it makes no difference whether this perception takes place in the physics laboratory or in the Christian Church. God has known all possible truth from eternity. We know truth because God graciously allows us to participate in the divine Logos. Christ is the word of God: he is the everlasting repository of all wisdom.[14]

Saving faith, faith as trust and commitment, is built on the foundation of generic faith, a resting of the mind in the sufficiency of the evidences.[15] Faith cannot authenticate itself through personal experience alone; it must make peace with the law of contradiction and empirical facts.

Carnell's type of apologetic was harder to uphold than more subjective types because it tended to force the theologian

into the role of a barrister whose duty it becomes to perpetually provide sufficient evidence for faith. Having
pitted his faith-perspective against other faith-perspectives
on the grounds of reason, this type of apologist may be too
easily dismissed in the minds of those whom his reason fails
to convince. They may, in fact, too easily disavow Christian
faith without ever having been confronted by its moral and
spiritual appeal.

One of the problems associated with Carnell's apologetic
was that the nature of his truth assumption tended to perpetuate the need for a defensive, polemical style of theology despite Carnell's attempts to overcome the polemical
tenor by making full use of the positive truths discovered
through general revelation. Karl Barth, no doubt, had
Carnell's style of theology in mind when he asserted that the
only true apologetic is the confrontation of unfaith by faith.[16]

Many modern forms of apologetics admit to no obligation
to philosophical criteria. Some such faith-perspectives rest
on the claim that it is Christian experience, not necessarily
rooted in historical events, which validates Christian truth.
Even if the objective forms of evidence could be removed by
critics, one could not, they contend, deny the reality of
that Christian experience which created the Christian Church.

But Carnell was not satisfied with this sort of subjectivity. If faith has no part with rational proof, the
heart is left with an unjustifiable bifurcation between
conventional laws of philosophy and the truth of revelation.

There is then no rational test for error. Carnell believed
that moral certainty cannot be separated from rational
certainty; certainty arises from the conviction that coherent truth is present.[17] Carnell's low regard for what
he considered to be "bad subjectivity" is indicated by
his identification of faith without rationality with the
epistemological thought forms of sectarian and occult
groups:

> . . .Faith without objectively verifiable truth
> is comparable to the sort of certainty which goes
> along with snake-handlers, sun-adorers, and
> esoteric faith-healing cults of sundry species. . .
> Faith must be founded in objectively verifiable
> metaphysical theories even if they fail to provide
> perfect demonstration. Apart from this, theology
> has no logic.[18]

Bad subjectivity follows whenever theologians divorce
the criterion of reason from personal experience. Carnell
asserted that truth is one, whether it be in philosophy,
science, or theology. The theologian has no right to
violate criteria for truth established by God. To do so
is to violate the canons of logic resident in the Logos
and in the common sense which governs our daily lives.

According to Carnell natural theology, with its
starting point in strict empiricism, is also inadequate
because it is impossible to account for our knowledge of
necessary truths on empiricist principles. Theology which
begins with an empirical starting point reduces knowledge
to opinion and, in many cases, to complete skepticism.

Until his death, Carnell persisted in his belief that revelation is meaningful only because God is rationally related to man, that God is the author of all truth, that rationality forms the univocal bond which significantly relates the two orders of being (natural and supernatural), and that it is through the criterion of reason that man can know with the consent of his intellectual faculties. Reason has its limits as a source of truth but not as a test for error.

In an age of science, Carnell's apologetic starting point was severely tested inasmuch as his a priori epistemology, combined with his view of Scripture as a revealed body of inerrant truth open to a full coherence test, obligated him logically and morally to the defense of objective and propositional biblical answers against which many scientists and philosophers presented contrary empirical evidence along with their a priori naturalistic biases. Such questions as creationism, the historicity of miracles, personal immortality, the trinitarian nature of God, incarnation and atonement, and the predestination and freedom questions are difficult, if not impossible, to prove on the basis of "systematic consistency" as Carnell defined it. But working within the realm of probable knowledge as the basis of all human decisions and compatible with the trustful certainty of faith, Carnell asserted that Christians can subject their truth claims to the canons of rationality operative in the larger human community and point to evidences supporting faith without depending solely on subjective experience or dogmatic authoritarianism. One cannot analyze the total apologetical work of Carnell without being struck by Carnell's persistent effort to remove the either/or choice between a faith inspired subjectivism or an external authoritarianism respecting the Christian revelation.

We must not be unfair to Carnell and leave the impression that faith was, for him, a matter of rationality alone. While he did defend the view that true philosophy and true theology cannot be fundamentally antithetical to each other, he did insist that faith is a coming into truth via the will. His was a balanced perspective. Faith involves trust in a reliable objective authority which would be unreasonable not to trust. But more importantly, faith involves an act of the will toward moral obedience. Philosophy may be the handmaiden of theology. It may test for error, but it can never lead into truth as moral rectitude.[19] Reason should not take us away from reality, and reality must not be limited to what one cogitates. Reality includes all that the existing individual experiences.[20] Science and philosophy are limited inasmuch as they can, by their epistemological methods, only account for reality as known by an ontological or propositional approach to truth. Faith as trust and commitment of the will (moral rectitude) leads into the richness and vitality of personal experience (knowledge by acquaintance), a virtual kingdom of love.

Carnell's apologetic was itself admittedly difficult to defend because of the nature of his apologetic norms, but, Carnell believed, it was one which allowed the man of faith to believe with the consent of all his faculties. Conservative Christianity should not be hastily judged before one has read Carnell. He has demonstrated that the conservative interpretation of Christianity is a live option in the twentieth century.

Footnotes

CHAPTER I

1. Ronald H. Nash, ed., The Case for Biblical Christianity (Grand Rapids, Mich.: Eerdmans Publishing Co., 1969),
p. 5.
2. The Case for Orthodox Theology (Philadelphia:
Westminister Press, 1959), p. 13.
3. Inaugural Address of Edward John Carnell, President
of Fuller Theological Seminary 1954-1959, delivered May 17,
1955 (published as a portion of the Carnell Memorial established in 1969-1970 by the Fuller Theological Seminary Alumni
Association; 135 North Oakland Ave., Pasadena, California,
91109).
4. Ibid.
5. Ibid.
6. Ibid.
7. Carnell's Introduction to Christian Apologetics was
selected as the winner in a competitive evangelical book a-
ward sponsored by Eerdmans Publishing Company. Henceforth
this work will be referred to as Apologetics in the footnotes.
8. Bernard Ramm, Types of Apologetic Systems (Wheaton,
Ill.: Van Kampen Press, 1953), p. 211.
9. Bernard Ramm, Varieties of Christian Apologetics
(Grand Rapids, Mich.: Baker Book House, 1961), p. 11
10. Ibid.
11. J.K.S. Reid, Christian Apologetics (Grand Rapids,
Mich.: Eerdmans, 1970), p. 15.
12. Ramm, Varieties, p. 13.
13. Alan Richardson, Christian Apologetics (New York:
Harper and Brothers, 1947), p. 7.
14. Ibid.
15. Reid, Christian Apologetics, p. 13. See also John
Macquarrie's Principles of Christian Theology, p. 35.
16. Ibid.
17. Ibid. For Barth's attitude toward apologetics see
his Church Dogmatics, Vo. I. Part I, Edinburgh, 1936, p. 31.
18. Ibid., p. 13, 14.
19. Ramm, Varieties, p. 13.

CHAPTER II

1. Richardson, Christian Apologetics, p. 19.

2. James Livingston, <u>Modern Christian Thought</u> (New York: Macmillan Co., 1971), p. 246.

3. Especially Harnack and, in America, Walter Rauschenbusch.

4. H. Richard Niebuhr, <u>Christ and Culture</u> (New York: Harper and Row, 1951), p. 83. Niebuhr says, "When Christianity deals with the problem of reason and revelation, what is ultimately in question is the relation of the revelation in Christ to the reason which prevails in culture" (p. 11).

5. This would include, according to Niebuhr, Abelard, Locke, Leibnitz, Kant, and Schleiermacher. See <u>Christ and Culture</u>, chapter three.

6. See Barth's <u>Protestant Theology in the Nineteenth Century</u>, 1974, chapter three.

7. H. Richard Niebuhr, p. 101.

8. See John C. Bennett, "A Changed Liberal -- But Still a Liberal," <u>The Christian Century</u>, LVI (Feb. 8, 1939), pp. 179-181

9. In his widely-acclaimed work, <u>God Was In Christ</u>, D.M. Baillie points out that the church had been haunted by docetism until modern times, pp. 11, 20. Liberals were quick to point out that their Christology was all the more significant because they had endeavored to take into full account the true and full humanity of Jesus.

10. H. Richard Niebuhr, p. 92.

11. Kenneth Cauthen, <u>The Impact of American Religious Liberalism</u> (New York: Harper and Row, 1962), p. 27.

12. Ibid., p. 29.

13. Livingston, p. 421.

14. Richardson, p. 55.

15. See Machen's <u>Christianity and Liberalism</u>, (Grand Rapids: Eerdmans, 1946).

16. Edward John Carnell, <u>The Theology of Reinhold Niebuhr</u> (Grand Rapids: Eerdmans, 1950), p. 22.

17. Ibid., p. 30.

18. Karl Barth published his <u>Epistle to the Romans</u> in 1919. In America an attack was sounded upon liberalism's ethical optimism by Reinhold Niebuhr's <u>Moral Man and Immoral Society</u> in 1932 and Edwin Lewis's <u>Christian Manifesto</u> was published in 1934. While all of these theologians stressed the importance of revelation, they disagreed as to how far one should withdraw from immanence and continuity. In general, American theologians were not as radical in their view of God's transcendence as continental theologians, particularly Barth.

19. "Dialectical" in this context refers to a theological method which involves the use of paradoxical language in talking about Christian revelation. The premise upon which the method is based is the "otherness" of God, the belief that no continuity or analogy exists between God and man.

20. <u>Fundamentalism</u> is a term that stands in need of definition. The word is used to denote the movement in American Protestantism which emphasized the importance of certain

fundamental doctrines such as the infallibility of the Bible,
Christ's Virgin Birth, his Substitutionary Atonement, Resurrection, and Second Coming. The importance of these fundament
doctrines was first emphasized by leaders of the movement thro
the publication of a series of ten small pamphlets called
The Fundamentals in 1910. Fundamentalism implies the view the
that there are certain irreducible truths in Christianity that
one must adhere to in order, to be a Christian. Norman F. Furn
The Fundamentalist Controversy, 1918-1931 (New Haven: Yale
University Press, 1954), p. 13. However, Carnell believed tha
the term also implies certain attitudes, a certain way of look
at life. Carnell sought to transcend fundamentalist attitudes
I believe that "conservative" best describes Carnell.

    21. See William E. Hordern's, A Layman's Guide to Protesta
Theology (London: Macmillan Co., 1969), p. 51.

    22. This is a term that is often used to describe Funda-
mentalists. But I find this term very inaccurate. Though
most fundamentalists believe in the verbal or plenary inspiration of Scripture, they do not consider that everything the
Bible says should be taken literally.

    23. This is likewise an unfair term to level against thos
of a more liberal persuasion. Much of the language used durin
the fundamentalist-liberal debate was polemical in tone and
implication.

    24. In addition to Carnell, the conservatives regarded
Carl Henry, Bernard Ramm, P.K. Jewett, Gordon Clark, S.J.
Mikolaski, R.V.G. Tasker, and Pierre Corthiel among their
leading scholars. See Christianity Today (January 1, 1965),
p. 26.

    25. Liberals usually considered those of a more conserva-
tive persuasion irrational because they accepted the authority
of the Bible without question or higher criticism. However,
the point is that conservatives have a different world view
than liberals. The liberal looks for natural causation of
supposed supernatural events. The conservative simply accepts
the reality of the supernatural God and of God's supernatural
intervention among men. But the conservative is not necessarily irrational. Given his world view, the conservative say
that things are rational, and that truth is established by
consistency and coherence. Conservatism could really be descri
as rationalism within Christianity. See Hordern's Layman's
Guide to Protestant Theology, pp. 51-72.

    26. The term "new theology" was not meant to imply that
the devotees of neo-orthodoxy had no continuity with theologians of the past. On the contrary, many believed that they
had rediscovered orthodoxy, particularly reformation theology.

    27. See Tillich's Systematic Theology I, p. 64 and
Bultmann's Jesus Christ and Mythology (New York: Charles
Scribner's Sons, 1958), p. 53.

28. Alan Richardson, "Reinhold Niebuhr as Apologist," Reinhold Niebuhr: His Religious, Social and Political Thought, ed. Charles W. Kegley and Robert W. Bretall (New York: Macmillan Co., 1956), p. 220.

29. Humanism may, of course, be defined in many ways. The term is used in this context to denote an attitude of mind which is sympathetic to human values and intolerant of unjustified impediments to their realization. See Reid, p. 183.

30. Reid, Christian Apologetics, p. 201.

31. Edward John Carnell, The Kingdom of Love and the Pride of Life (Grand Rapids, Mich.: Eerdmans Publishing Co., 1960), p. 9.

32. Many theologians do, however, regard a priori thinking presumptuous because they believe it sets up false criteria by which to judge revelation. Kierkegaard and Barth were particularly antagonistic toward an a priori judging of revelation. Sympathetic toward their views, William Hordern severely criticized Carnell for "setting up a priori categories for God to fulfill." See Hordern's New Reformation Theology, pp. 78-83. For somewhat different reasons, biblical dogmatists like Gordon Clark and Cornelius Van Til also oppose an a priori judging of revelation. See Clark's Three Types of Religious Philosophy and Van Til's Defense of the Faith.

33. Edward John Carnell, Christian Commitment (New York: Macmillan Co., 1957), p. 142.

34. Kingdom of Love, p. 6.

35. Paul Tillich, "The Problem of Theological Method," Four Existentialist Theologians, ed. Will Herberg (Doubleday Anchor Books, 1958), p. 253.

36. Carnell criticized Tillich particularly for preferring speculation to exegesis, for surrendering objective elements in faith, and for making unjustified concessions to philosophy and science in an attempt to describe structures and categories of being and the logos in which being becomes manifest. See Kingdom of Love, pp. 8-9.

37. Richardson, Christian Apologetics, p. 24.

38. Apologetic theology presupposes an analogia entis, an analogy of being between God and man. this is not to say, however, that theologians like Luther and Barth, who demonstrated a profound distrust of philosophy, have no apologetic worth. Luther and Barth refused to separate God's being from God's acting in Jesus Christ. Consequently their apologetic is closely related to their Christology.

39. Richardson, p. 27.

40. Apologetics, p. 121.

41. Richardson, p. 26.

42. Ibid., p. 27, 28.

43. Carnell did not, of course, admit to their discovering all the truths of special revelation. But he did present special revelation as a fulfillment of natural truth, not as a negation.

44. Kingdom of Love, p. 9.

45. Ibid.

46. Ibid., p. 6.

47. The Case For Orthodox Theology, p. 119.
48. Ibid.
49. Ibid.
50. Kingdom of Love, p. 9.
51. See H. Richard Niebuhr's Christ and Culture (New York: Harper and Row, 1956), Chapters II, VI.
52. Edward John Carnell, "Post-Fundamentalist Faith," The Christian Century, August 26, 1959, p. 971.
53. See Paul Tillich's Systematic Theology I (Chicago: University of Chicago Press, 1951), p. 14.
54. These books are the primary sources used for our treatment of Carnell.
55. Nash, The Case for Biblical Christianity, p. 6.
56. Richardson, p. 38.
57. Ibid.
58. Ibid.
59. Ibid., p. 39.
60. Carnell believed that these are the four essential aspects of man's nature, and that Christianity fulfills the essential needs of each. Much of Carnell's work was devoted to a correlation of Christianity with the needs and concerns raised in each of these environmental spheres. See Christian Commitment, p. 286.
61. Edward John Carnell, A Philosophy of the Christian Religion (Grand Rapids, Mich.: Eerdmans Publishing Co., 1952), p. 450f. Henceforth this work will be referred to as Philosophy in the footnotes.
62. Ibid., p. 453.
63. Ibid., P. 179.
64. See chapters ten and eleven of Carnell's Christian Commitment.
65. Kierkegaard would not have agreed with Carnell's view that God and man share a common moral and spiritual environment. Nor would he have agreed with Carnell's emphasis upon the moral realm of existence; the highest mode of existence for Kierkegaard was the religious. Kierkegaard feared immanence more than any other view of Christianity. See Kierkegaard's Concluding Unscientific Postscript, trans. by Walter Lowrie (Princeton, New Jersey: Princeton Univ. Press, 1945), pp. 507-508.
        Interestingly enough, William Hordern's criticism of Christian Commitment was that it threatened to replay the error associated with an undue emphasis on God's immanence, a criticism most often offered against theological liberalism. See Hordern's Case for a New Reformation Theology (Philadelphia: Westminister Press, 1959), p. 105.
66. Nash, The Case for Biblical Christianity, p. 8.
67. Carnell, "Post-Fundamentalist Faith," p. 971.
68. Edward John Carnell, "A Proposal to Reinhold Niebuhr, The Christian Century, October 17, 1956, p. 1199.
69. Carnell distinguished between Christ's "active" and "passive" obedience. The former consisted in a perfect fulfillment of righteousness (there was no gap between what Christ was and what he ought to be); the latter consisted in his substitutionary death on the cross. Carnell believed that good use had been made of Christ's active righteousness (love) by modern apologists, but that the latter emphasis,

the imputed righteousness of Christ, had been neglected.
See Christian Commitment, pp. 249-251.
70. Kingdom of Love, pp. 7, 8.
71. Ibid., p. 9.

CHAPTER III

1. Apologetics, p. 23.
2. Ibid., p. 19.
3. Ibid., p. 29.
4. Ibid., p. 7.
5. Ibid., p. 353.
6. Ibid., p. 45.
7. Ibid., pp. 24, 25.
8. Ibid., p. 354.
9. Bernard Ramm, "Systems Stressing Revelation,"
Types of Apologetic Systems (Wheaton, Ill.: Van Kampen Press,
1953), p. 228.
10. Ronald H. Nash, "Philosophical Apologetics," The
New Evangelicalism (Grand Rapids, Mich.: Zondervan, 1963), p. 115.
11. Ibid.
12. Many significant works on apologetics, with similar
interests and methodologies, have been published by evangelicals
since the end of World War II. Edward John Carnell, Carl Henry,
Bernard Ramm, and Gordon Clark have all used the presuppositionalist method. And more recently, John Warick Montgomery and
Francis Schaeffer have demonstrated similar concerns. Evangelicals are also fond of claiming C.S. Lewis as a Christian
writer with interests similar to their own.
13. See Nash, The New Evangelicalism, Chapters 8 and 9.
14. Ibid., pp. 127, 128.
15. A judgment is to be trusted when it accords with the
facts of our experience. By "experience" Carnell means that
"total breadth of human consciousness which embraces the entire rational, volitional, and emotional life of man, both within
and without." See Apologetics, p. 56.
16. Apologetics, p. 298.
17. See Nash, The New Evangelicalism, Chapter 9.
18. Ramm, Types, p. 180.
19. Gordon H. Clark, Christian View of Men and Things
(Grand Rapids, Mich.: Eerdmans, 1952), p. 29.
20. Ibid.
21. Ibid., p. 30.
22. Ibid., p. 31.
23. Ibid., p. 32.
24. Ibid., p. 33.
25. Ibid.
26. Ibid, p. 34.

27. Apologetics, p. 89.
28. Nash, The New Evangelicalism. p. 126.
29. Apologetics, p. 91.
30. Ibid., p. 90.
31. Ibid., p. 96.
32. Ibid., p. 47.
33. Ibid.
34. Ibid., p. 63.
35. Ibid., pp. 56, 57.
36. Ibid., pp. 60, 61.
37. See Carnell, Apologetics, pp. 46-67, for a fuller explanation. More space was devoted to pragmatism because of its deep rootage in American thought.
38. Apologetics, p. 56.
39. Ibid., p. 61.
40. Ibid., p. 63.
41. Ibid.
42. See Edgar Sheffield Brightman's A Philosophy of Religion (New York: Prentice Hall, Inc., 1947), pp. 126-129.
43. Clark, Three Types of Religious Philosophy, p. 106.
44. See Brightman, A Philosophy of Religion, pp. 175-178.
45. Clark, Three Types of Religious Philosophy, pp. 107-1:
46. Ibid., p. 123.
47. Ibid., p. 125.
48. Ibid., p. 66.
49. Cornelius Van Til, The Defense of the Faith (Philadelp The Presbyterian and Reformed Publishing Co., 1955), pp. 264-26
50. Edward John Carnell, Review of The Defense of the Faith, by Cornelius Van Til, The Christian Century, January 4, 1956. pp. 14-15.
51. Ibid.
52. Ibid.
53. Ramm, Types, p. 215.
54. Nash, ed., The Case for Biblical Christianity, p. 51.
55. Ibid., p. 53.
56. Ibid., p. 54.
57. Apologetics, p. 65.
58. Ibid., p. 66.
59. Ibid., p. 68. Carnell is here quoting from Calvin.
60. This criticism is at least implied by Reinhold Niebuhr See Charles W. Kegley and Robert W. Bretall, eds., "Reply to Interpretation and Criticism," Reinhold Niebuhr: His Religious Social, and Political Thought (New York: Macmillan Co., 1967), p. 443.
61. Apologetics, p. 70.
62. Ibid., p. 68.
63. Carl Henry, ed., Revelation and the Bible (Grand Rapid Mich.: Baker Book House, 1958), p. 37.
64. Ibid.
65. Ibid., p. 36.

66. David L. Barr, "Becoming A Christian: A Preliminary Examination of Kierkegaard's Training in Christianity" (unpublished paper, Dept. of Religion, Florida State University, 1969), p. 15.

67. Ibid., pp. 9, 10.

68. Henry, ed., Revelation and the Bible, p. 37.

69. Ibid., p. 36.

70. Apologetics, p. 47.

71. Søren Kierkegaard, Training in Christianity, trans. Walter Lowrie (Princeton: Princeton University Press, 1944), p. 201.

72. By "existential communication" Kierkegaard means that Christianity is not a doctrine but an existential communication expressing an existential contradiction.

73. Ramm, Types, p. 57.

74. Apologetics, p. 63. It is important to understand what Carnell meant by univocal and how he used the term. "Terms may be used in one of three ways: with one meaning (univocally), with different meanings (equivocally), and with a proportional meaning--partly the same, partly different (analogically)." See Apologetics, p. 144.

75. Ramm, Types, p. 215.

76. Apologetics, p. 162.

77. Ibid., see pp. 147-151.

78. Ibid., see footnote on p. 151.

79. Ibid., p. 139.

80. Ibid., p. 124.

81. Ibid., p. 125. Carnell says little about what he means by these terms, other than what has already been said in the above paragraphs.

82. Clark, in Revelation and the Bible, ed. by Henry, p. 33.

83. Apologetics, p. 139.

84. Ibid., p. 129.

85. Ibid., p. 152.

86. Ibid., p. 125.

87. Ibid., pp. 158, 159.

88. Ibid., p. 159.

89. Ibid., p. 165.

90. Ibid., p. 167.

91. Ramm, Types, pp. 225, 226.

92. Apologetics, see note, p. 151.

93. Ibid.

94. Ibid., see note, p. 149.

95. Ibid., p. 173.

96. Ramm, Types, p. 11.

97. Apologetics, p. 157.

98. Ibid., p. 175.

99. Ibid., p. 178.

100. Ibid., p. 210.

101. Ibid., p. 7.

102. Ibid., p. 354.

103. Ibid.
104. Ibid.
105. Ibid., p. 355.
106. Ibid., p. 356.
107. Ibid. All of these problems are important, and Carnell discusses them at length in An Introduction to Christia Apologetics. I have purposely avoided treating them because I do not believe they would serve our purpose at this point.
108. Ibid., p. 357.

CHAPTER IV

1. The "heart" is a term used throughout this chapter to denote the complex man: body, spirit, and whatever else forms the totality of human nature.
2. Consistency, for Carnell, means conformity to the law of contradiction, and it is the surest test for the absence of truth.
3. Carnell, Philosophy, p. 184.
4. Ibid., p. 209.
5. Ibid., p. 210.
6. Ibid., p. 38.
7. Ibid., p. 39.
8. Ramm, Types, p. 216.
9. Philosophy, p. 450.
10. Ibid., p. 452.
11. Ibid., p. 453.
12. Ibid., p. 179.
13. Ibid., p. 181.
14. Ramm, Types, p. 219.
15. Philosophy, p. 457.
16. Ibid., p. 494.
17. Ibid., p. 507.
18. Ibid., p. 495.
19. Ibid., p. 505.
20. Ibid., p. 506.
21. Ibid.
22. Ramm, Types, pp. 211, 212.
23. Carnell stated that "the law of self-preservation is so deeply engrained in our nature that it is impossible for man to engage in any conscious activity without seeking his own well-being." Philosophy, p. 15.
24. Ibid., p. 21.
25. Ibid.
26. Ibid., p. 19.
27. Ibid.
28. Ibid., p. 82.
29. Ibid., p. 84.
30. Ibid., pp. 97-98
31. Philosophy, p. 115, citing Reinhold Niebuhr, Beyond Tragedy (New York: Charles Scribner's Sons, 1937), p. 94.
32. Philosophy, p. 117.
33. Ibid., p. 117.
34. Ibid., p. 178.
35. Ibid., p. 156.

36. Ibid., pp. 162, 163.
37. Ibid., p. 178.
38. Ibid.
39. Ibid., p. 175.
40. Ibid., p. 178.
41. Ibid., p. 223.
42. Ibid., p. 181.
43. Ibid.
44. Ibid., p. 179.
45. Ibid., p. 233.
46. Corliss Lamont, Humanism as a Philosophy (New York: Philosophical Library, 1949), p. 20, in Philosophy, p. 233.
47. Philosophy, p. 229. "The ethic of Christianity is based on what is conventionally known as the two tables of the law. The first four of the Ten Commandments summarize man's duty to God, while the last six detail the relations which should subsist between men," p. 227.
48. Ibid.
49. Ibid., p. 239.
50. Ibid., p. 240.
51. Ibid., p. 243.
52. Lamont, p. 297.
53. Philosophy, p. 254.
54. Søren Kierkegaard, Concluding Unscientific Postscript (Princeton: Princeton University Press, 1941), p. 281.
55. Reinhold Niebuhr, Human Destiny (New York: Charles Scribner's Sons, 1946), p. 108.
56. Philosophy, pp. 272, 273.
57. Ibid., pp. 293, 294.
58. Ibid., p. 326.
59. Ibid., p. 327.
60. Ibid., pp. 328, 329.
61. Ibid., p. 511.
62. Christianity seeks to more fully satisfy, not denounce, those values which all men seek by nature, such as pleasure, economic-security, wisdom, etc., Ibid., p. 513.
63. Philosophy, p. 452.
64. Ibid., p. 453.
65. Ibid., p. 455.
66. Ibid., p. 453.
67. Ibid., p. 473.
68. Carnell, Burden of Søren Kierkegaard, p. 117, citing Kierkegaard, Philosophical Fragments, p. 79.
69. Søren Kierkegaard, Philosophical Fragments, trans. David Swenson (Princeton: Princeton University Press, 1969), p. 61.
70. Carnell, Burden of Søren Kierkegaard, p. 84.
71. Ibid., p. 133.
72. Ibid., p. 167.
73. Ibid., p. 166.

168

74. Philosophy, p. 452.
75. Ibid., p. 450.
76. Ibid., p. 494.
77. Apologetics, p. 8.
78. Philosophy, p. 512.
79. Ibid.

CHAPTER V

1. Carnell, The Kingdom of Love, p. 9.
2. Carnell, Christian Commitment, p. 198.
3. See Niebuhr's typologies in Christ and Culture.
4. See The Kingdom of Love and the Pride of Life and an article entitled "Orthodoxy: Cultic vs. Classical" in the March 30, 1960 edition of Christian Century.
5. Carnell, Kingdom of Love, p. 6.
6. Ibid., p. 9.
7. By "human self-sufficiency" Carnell had in mind attempts such as Thomas Aquinas' to apprehend God by means of rational dialectic, such as the famous "five proofs."
8. Carnell, Christian Commitment, p. 73.
9. Carnell, The Burden of Søren Kierkegaard, p. 56.
10. By "propositional truth" Carnell meant "judgments which conceptually house the real." "Ontological truth" is true to the extent that something participates in being. See Christian Commitment, p. 14.
11. Søren Kierkegaard, Stages on Life's Way, trans. Walter Lowrie, Harper Torchbooks (New York: Harper and Row, 1945), p.
12. Christian Commitment, p. 73.
13. Ibid., p. 16.
14. See Walter Lowrie's translation of The Concept of Dread, p. 39. "Man as soul is that animating faculty -- generally known by its association with free conduct -- which separates living creatures from pure matter." See Burden of Søren Kierkegaard, p. 45.
15. Carnell, like Niebuhr and Kierkegaard, realized that it was extremely difficult to maintain a satisfactory balance between necessity and possibility.
16. Christian Commitment, p. 21.
17. Ibid., p. 22. For Kierkegaard, the religious mode of existence is made possible because God moves from outside oneself.
18. William Hordern, Review of Christian Commitment, by Edward John Carnell, Christian Century, LXXIV (Sept. 4, 1957), 1041-1042.
19. Christian Commitment, p. 91.
20. Ibid., p. 73.
21. Burden of Søren Kierkegaard, p. 51.
22. Kierkegaard, Concluding Unscientific Postscript, pp. 186-188.

23. Burden of Søren Kierkegaard, p. 52.
24. Christian Commitment, p. 139. Carnell's way
of talking about God would, of course, be too "logical" and
"metaphysical" for Kierkegaard. For Kierkegaard, God is
the One through whom one finds selfhood; God is not seen as
a metaphysical entity.
25. Ibid., p. 135.
26. Ibid., p. 138. Compare this view of immanence with
Kierkegaard's radical transcendence of God.
27. Ibid.
28. An Examination of Sir William Hamilton's Philosophy
(New York: Longmans, Green and Co., 1889), pp. 127-128.
Kierkegaard would not accept this statement.
29. Christian Commitment, p. 131. Nor would Kierkegaard
accept this.
30. Burden of Søren Kierkegaard, p. 170.
31. Christian Commitment, p. 141.
32. Hordern, p. 1042.
33. I have in mind many reformed theologians who make
God the only interpretation, the final reference point in
human predication. In this view, one can only think God's
thoughts after Him. To discover and follow God's interpretations
is to think analogically. Carnell contends that man shares in the
life of God whenever he makes contact with ultimate elements
in either the rational, aesthetic, or moral and spiritual
environment; knowledge is possible because of the Imago Dei.
34. Burden of Søren Kierkegaard, pp. 52, 53.
35. Christian Commitment, p. 69.
36. Ibid., p. 110.
37. Ibid.
38. Ibid., p. 112.
39. Ibid., p. 70.
40. Burden of Søren Kierkegaard. p. 167.
41. Ibid.
42. Ibid.
43. Christian Commitment, p. 205.
44. Carnell, The Theology of Reinhold Niebuhr, pp. 215-243.
45. Reinhold Niebuhr, An Interpretation of Christian
Ethics (New York: Harper and Brothers, 1935), p. 51.
46. Christian Commitment, p. 293.
47. Ibid., p.208.
48. Ibid., p. 210.
49. Ibid., p. 212.
50. Ibid., p. 240. Kierkegaard would have agreed.
51. Ibid. Kierkegaard would not have agreed.
52. Ibid. The prerequisite to an acquaintance knowledge
of God is humility. Repentance is an expression of humility.
Concerning the problem of evil, Carnell says that one must
first face the problem of sin and the aroused judicial sentiment of God before he has the right to inquire into this problem. Upon doing so, love and trust replace suspicion and fear.
See p. 269f. For Kierkegaard, however, repentance is a movement within the immanent.

53. Ibid., p. 158.
54. Ibid., p. 250.
55. Carnell, The Kingdom of Love, p. 17. This sounds very Kierkegaardian.
56. Kierkegaard, Works of Love, p. 5.
57. Ibid., pp. 81, 82.
58. Burden of Søren Kierkegaard, p. 124.
59. Ibid., p. 164.
60. Christian Commitment, p. 303.
61. Ibid.
62. Ibid., p. 302.

CHAPTER VI

1. Evangelicals have been somewhat sensitive about this accusation as well as the general depreciation for reason in modern thought and culture.
2. The term "eclectic" has here no invidious connotation. It is used to simply point out that Carnell selected truths from various religious philosophies which he believed to be relevant for Christian apologetics.
3. Edward John Carnell, Review of The Case for a New Reformation Theology, by William Hordern; The Case for Theology in a Liberal Perspective, by L. Harold Dewolf, Journal of Bible and Religion, XXVII (October, 1959), p. 319.
4. William Hordern and L. Harold DeWolf, Review of The Case for Orthodox Theology, by Edward John Carnell, Journal of Bible and Religion, XXVII (October, 1959), p. 315.
5. Ibid., p. 316.
6. Ibid., p. 314.
7. William Hordern, Review of Christian Commitment by Edward John Carnell, Christian Century, Sept. 4, 1957. It is noteworthy to mention that Hordern takes the work of conservative theologians more seriously than most nonconservatives. In Chapter three of his book, A Layman's Guide to Protestant Theology, Hordern gives some treatment of Carnell, his work, and his place in protestant theology.
8. See Hordern's and DeWolf's review of The Case for Orthodox Theology.
9. A quotation from Menninger cited by the novelist Chaim Potok, The Chosen (Greenwich, Conn.: Fawcett Publications, Inc., 1967), p. 4.
10. Gresham Machen, Christianity and Liberalism (Grand Rapids, Mich.: Eerdmans, 1923), p. 160.
11. See Ronald H. Nash, The New Evangelicalism (Grand Rapids, Mich.: Zondervan Publishing Co., 1963), pp. 88-91.
12. Christian Commitment, p. 269.
13. Ibid., p. 268.
14. Ibid., p. 269.
15. Ibid., p. 267.
16. See Barth's Doctrine of the Word of God; Church Dogmatics, Vol. I, Part I, Eng. trans. by G.T. Thomson, Edinburgh, 1936. pp. 30-33.
17. Apologetics, p. 117.

18. Ibid.
19. Christian Commitment, p. 15f.
20. Kingdom of Love, p. 38.

Selected Edward John Carnell Bibliography

Books

The Burden of Søren Kierkegaard. Grand Rapids, Michigan: William B. Eerdmans Publishing Co., 1956.

The Case for Biblical Christianity. Grand Rapids, Michigan: William B. Eerdmans Publishing Co., 1969.

The Case for Orthodox Theology. Philadelphia: Westminister Press, 1959.

Christian Commitment. New York: Macmillan Co., 1957.

An Introduction to Christian Apologetics. Grand Rapids, Michigan: William B. Eerdmans Publishing Co., 1948.

The Kingdom of Love and the Pride of Life. Grand Rapids, Michigan: William B. Eerdmans Publishing Co., 1960.

A Philosophy of the Christian Religion. Grand Rapids, Michigan: William B. Eerdmans Publishing Co., 1952.

Television: Servant or Master? Grand Rapids, Michigan: William B. Eerdmans Publishing Co., 1950.

The Theology of Reinhold Niebuhr. Grand Rapids, Michigan: William B. Eerdmans Publishing Co., 1950.

Chapters in Books

"Niebuhr's Criteria of Verification," Chapter 18 in Reinhold Niebuhr: His Religious, Social, and Political Thought, Ed. Charles W. Kegley and Robert W. Bretall. Vol. II of the Library of Living Theology, The Macmillan Co., 1956. pp. 379-380.

"Reinhold Niebuhr's View of Scripture," Chapter IX in Inspiration and Interpretation, Ed. John F. Walvoord, William B. Eerdmans Co., 1957. pp. 239-252.

"Fundamentalism," Chapter 37 in Handbook of Christian Theology, Meridian Books, 1958. pp. 142-143.

A Chapter in How My Mind Has Changed, Ed. Harold E. Fey,
Meridian Books, 1960. pp. 91-104.

"The Government of the Church," Chapter 37, Basic Christian
Doctrines, Carl F.H. Henry, Ed., Holt, Rinehart, and
Winston, Inc., 1962. pp. 248-254.

"The Son of God," Chapter 14, in The Empirical Theology of
Henry Nelson Wieman, Ed. Robert W. Bretall. Vol. IV
of the Library of Living Theology, The Macmillan Co.,
1963. pp. 306-314.

Articles

"Why Neo-Orthodoxy?" The Watchman-Examiner, February 19,
1948. pp. 180-181.

"Is Drunkeness a Sin?" United Evangelical Action, March 1,
1948. pp. 6, 8.

"How Every Christian Can Defend His Faith," Moody Monthly,
(Part One) January, 1950. pp. 312-312, 343. (Part
Two) February, 1950. pp. 384-385, 429-431; (Part
Three) March, 1950. pp. 460-461, 506-507.

"The Problem of Religious Authority," His, February, 1950.
pp. 6-9, 11-12.

"The Christian and Television," His, May, 1950. pp. 1-3, 6.

"Should a Christian Go to War?" His, April, 1951. pp. 4-8, 10.

"The Grave Peril of Provincializing Jesus," The Pulpit, May,
1951. pp. 2-4. Reprinted in the Presbyterian Outlook,
March 31, 1952. pp. 5-6.

"Beware of the 'New Deism'," His, December, 1951. pp. 14-16,
35-36.

"A Proposal to Reinhold Niebuhr," The Christian Century,
October 17, 1956. pp. 1197-1199.

"The Nature of the Unity We Seek," Religion in Life, Spring,
1957. pp. 191-199.

"Can Billy Graham Slay the Giant?" Christianity Today, May
13, 1957. pp. 3-5.

"Billy Graham and the Pope's Legions," Christianity Today,
July 22, 1957. pp. 20-21.

"Personal Happiness and Prosperity," Christian Economics,
September 3, 1957. p. 4.

"Orthodoxy and Ecumenism," Christianity Today, September 1, 1958. pp. 15-18, 24.

"Post-Fundamentalist Faith," The Christian Century, August 26, 1959. p. 971.

"The Virgin Birth of Christ," Christianity Today, December 7, 1959. pp. 9-10.

"Jesus Christ and Man's Condition," Encounter, Vol. 21, No. 1; Winter, 1960. pp. 52-58.

"Orthodoxy: Cultic vs. Classical," The Christian Century, March 30, 1960. pp. 377-399.

"A Layman's Dictionary of Theology," Christian Herald, July, 1960. pp. 57-58.

"Evil-Why?" Eternity, December, 1960. pp. 22-24, 31.

"A Discussion of Capital Punishment," Eternity, June, 1961. pp. 19-20, 32.

'The Secret of Loving Your Neighbor," Eternity, 1961. pp. 15-16

'Barth as Inconsistent Evangelical," The Christian Century, June 6, 1962. pp. 713-714.

'The Government of the Church," Christianity Today, June 22, 1962. pp. 18-19.

'The Fear of Death," The Christian Century, January 30, 1963. pp. 136-137.

'A Christian Social Ethics," The Christian Century, August 7, 19 pp. 979-980.

'Goldwater: Yes or No?" (contribution to symposium), The Christian Century, July 8, 1964. p. 881.

'Conservatives and Liberals Do Not Need Each Other," Christianity Today, May 21, 1965. pp. 874-876.

Other

Inaugural Address of Edward John Carnell, President of Fuller Theological Seminary 1954-1959, delivered May 17, 1955 (published as a portion of the Carnell Memorial established in 1969-1970 by the Fuller Theological Seminary Alumni Association; 135 North Oakland Ave., Pasadena, Calif., 91109).

Material About Carnell

Critical and Biographical

Barnhart, J.E. "The Religious Epistemology and Theodicy
of Edward John Carnell and Edgar Sheffield Brightman."
Unpublished Ph.D. dissertation, Boston University, 1964.

Haines, Aubrey B. "Edward John Carnell: An Evaluation."
Christian Century, June 7, 1967. p. 751.

Hordern, William, and DeWolf, Harold L. Review of The Case
for Orthodox Theology, by Edward John Carnell, Journal of
Bible and Religion, October, 1959. pp. 311-317.

Nash, Ronald H. The New Evangelicalism. Grand Rapids,
Michigan: Zondervan Publishing Co., 1963.

Ramm, Bernard. Types of Apologetic Systems. Wheaton,
Illinois: Van Kampen Press, 1953.

Sailer, William S. "The Role of Reason in the Theologies
of Nel Ferre and Edward John Carnell." Unpublished
S.T.D. dissertation, Temple University, 1964.

Sims, John A. "The Apologetical Odyssey of Edward John
Carnell." Unpublished M.A. thesis, Florida State
University, 1971.

_____. "The Problem of Knowledge in the Apologetical
Concerns of Edwin Lewis and Edward John Carnell."
Unpublished Ph.D. dissertation, Florida State
University, 1975.